JEREMY TAYLOR
1700–1976

GARLAND REFERENCE LIBRARY
OF THE HUMANITIES
(VOL. 177)

JEREMY TAYLOR
1700–1976
An Annotated Checklist

compiled by
William P. Williams

GARLAND PUBLISHING, INC. • NEW YORK & LONDON
1979

Library of Congress Cataloging in Publication Data

Williams, William Proctor, 1939–
  Jeremy Taylor, 1700–1976.

  (Garland reference library of the humanities ; v. 177)
  Includes indexes.
  1. Taylor, Jeremy, Bp. of Down and Connor,
1613–1667—Bibliography.   2. Theology—17th
century—Bibliography.   3. Theology, Anglican—
Bibliography.   I. Title.
Z8861.8.W54   [BX5199.T3]   016.283'092'4   [B]
ISBN 0-8240-9756-4   78-68302

Printed on acid-free, 250-year-life paper
Manufactured in the United States of America

to Karen, Elizabeth, and William

CONTENTS

INTRODUCTION

Jeremy Taylor was born at Cambridge in 1613 and was baptized on 15 August in Holy Trinity Church. His father, Nathaniel, a barber-surgeon, was churchwarden of that parish, and although there appears to be some dispute about the family's exact residence (see No. 251), it is certain that Taylor entered Perse School, a grammar school recently founded by Dr. Perse, and that he entered Gonville and Caius College, Cambridge, in 1626, initially as a sizar but from 1628 until 1631 holding a bursary established by the same Dr. Perse. He proceeded B.A. in 1631 and M.A. in 1633, also taking holy orders in the latter year. After receiving his M.A. he was appointed Reader in Rhetoric by the Master of Gonville and Caius, Richard Batchcroft, his former tutor.

In 1633 or 1634 Taylor took the place of a friend to preach at St. Paul's Cathedral, where one of his auditors was William Laud, Archbishop of Canterbury. Laud was so impressed with Taylor's preaching that he immediately began to take an interest in his career and forced Taylor's election to a fellowship at All Souls College, Oxford, in 1635. Laud made him one of his own chaplains and subsequently a chaplain of King Charles I. He preached the annual Gunpowder Treason sermon in 1638 at St. Mary's, the university church, and this became his first published work. In the following year he was given the living at Uppingham, Rutlandshire, and since his marriage in this year had deprived him of his All Souls fellowship, it appears that he spent the next three years in his parish and that he took the job of parish priest seriously. In 1642 he left Uppingham to join the king at Oxford. He was not ejected from his living but left voluntarily, joining the king as one of his chaplains. He brought with him the manuscript of his *Sacred Order of Episcopacy* which so pleased the king that the degree D.D. was conferred on Taylor by Oxford by royal command on 1 November 1642. Taylor was in Oxford from that date until late in 1644, and during his time there he became acquainted with the royalist intellectual circle headed by Lucius Carey, Lord Falkland, and centered at Falkland's home, Great Tew, north of Oxford. Other members of this circle included William Chillingworth, Henry Hammond, and Christopher Hatton, and it was the latter who was to become Taylor's friend and patron.

Taylor seems to have also served as a chaplain to the royalist armies, for in December of 1644 he was taken prisoner after the battle for Cardigan Castle in Wales. We do not know how or when he was released, but when he did gain his freedom he chose to settle in Wales and spent nearly a decade of his life there. In the spring of 1645 he kept a school with William Wyatt, and shortly afterward became the chaplain to Richard Vaughn, 2nd Earl of Carbery, at Golden Grove in Carmarthensire. During his time in Lord Carbery's service Taylor produced nearly all those works which brought him fame. He wrote two very controversial works—at least, controversial at the time—*The Liberty of Prophesying* (1647) and *Unum Necessarium* (1655). The earlier work is a plea for toleration of religion and the second an argument about Original Sin in which Taylor holds rather unorthodox, perhaps even Pelagian views. Both works were able to produce wrath and rejection as late as this century as is witnessed by Nos. 287, 373, 376, 406, and 414 in this bibliography. He also produced the two devotional works which are his most noted writings, *Holy Living* and *Holy Dying* (1650 and 1651). Both works were written for Francis, Countess of Carbery, although she died before the last one was printed, and they have never ceased to be manuals of devotion in popular use among the laity. These, and the year-long series of sermons eventually collected under the title of *Eniautos* (1653), have also been the material used either to make the grand and sweeping claims for Taylor as a stylist or to damn him as an unintellectual writer of purple rhetoric. Most of the items of general literary criticism in this bibliography represent one or the other of these extremes and seldom does one encounter a more moderate and reasonable view. However, these were not the only works Taylor published while at Golden Grove. He also published a much neglected and splendid life of Christ, *The Great Exemplar* (1649); a substitute for the Book of Common Prayer which had been abolished by Parliament, *The Golden Grove* (1654); another controversial work, *The Real Presence* (1654); and several others.

However, Taylor, having fallen afoul not only of the authority of Parliament by being employed as a private chaplain to Lord Carbery in contravention of Cromwell's order of 24 November 1655 against the activities of sequestered clerics, but also of his own Anglican party because of the opinions expressed in *The Liberty of Prophesying* and *Unum Necessarium*, was imprisoned late in 1655 in Chepstow Castle. We do not know the exact reason for this imprisonment, but in March of 1656 when he was released he went to London, probably to minister to the underground Anglican congregations there, and did not again return to Wales. One other connection with the west country was his membership in the circle surrounding Katharine Phillips, "The Matchless Orinda," and this is memorialized in his *A Discourse of Friendship* (1657), one of his most charming and human works.

Taylor's "parishoners" in London included John Evelyn, and for our knowledge of Taylor's activities from 1655 to 1661 we are almost entirely indebted to Evelyn's meticulous recording of events (see Nos. 265 and 266). In 1658 Taylor published *A Collection of Offices*; because this work was blatantly a substitute Prayer Book and because its frontispiece depicted Christ in an attitude of prayer contrary to a recent law, he was sent to the Tower. He was there only a short time and later in 1658 he was taken up by a new patron, Edward, Lord Conway. Aside from Ragley, Warwickshire, the Conways had estates in the north of Ireland, and Edward, the 3rd Viscount, was an ardent royalist and Anglican. Late in 1658 Taylor was given the position of chaplain to the family at their home in Portmore, in Ulster, and he was also appointed to the position of assistant lecturer at the parish church in Lisburn. Even before his arrival in Ireland, the Ulster Presbyterians began an assault on his person and character, eventually securing a warrant for his arrest and transportation to Dublin to answer for his offenses in November 1659, but he was soon released. Presumably his crime was no more than his being an Anglican.

In the spring of 1660 Taylor traveled to London and was present at the return of the king on 29 May 1660. He dedicated to Charles II what he considered his masterpiece, *Ductor Dubitantium* (1660), a huge manual of casuistry, and he dedicated to Mary of Orange his *Worthy Communicant* (1660). Taylor had offered these two books to the Stuarts as further demonstrations of his loyalty and service and it seems clear he expected a reward. However, Gilbert Sheldon, a man distrustful of Taylor and his doctrine, was the real power behind the aged Archbishop of Canterbury, William Juxon, and it was probably Sheldon who sent Taylor back to Ireland as Bishop of Down and Connor. It was bad enough not to be rewarded with an English bishopric, no matter how insignificant, but Taylor was sent back among the very people who had secured his arrest and transportation to Dublin barely one year before. However, upon the recommendation of the Duke of Ormonde, he was appointed Vice-Chancellor of Trinity College, Dublin, and into this task, which required the entire reorganization of the college, Taylor threw himself vigorously.

Taylor's attempts to regularize the clergy in his diocese, his assumption that the church was established according to law, and his efforts to ensure that the holders of livings within his see were properly ordained have led to charges being raised that all his notions of toleration and fair play as set forth in *The Liberty of Prophesying* were repudiated by his conduct after the Restoration (see especially Nos. 287, 303, 305, 414, 421). Although the remainder of Taylor's life was spent in rather unpleasant disputes within his diocese, he did much to assure the establishment of the Anglican church in Northern Ireland, and devoted himself to restoring the fabric of his cathedral and of parish churches. In the summer of 1667 he visited a fever patient, caught the disease, and died on 13 August. He was buried in the cathedral he had done so much to build in Dromore on 3 September.

• • •

For a Caroline divine and an acknowledged prose stylist, Jeremy Taylor has suffered a curious neglect. His works, even minor ones, were frequently reprinted in the eighteenth and nineteenth centuries and the greatest number of entries in this bibliography from those two centuries record the regular republication of his works or their collection or abridgment. Many writers of those two centuries cited him either on points of style or belief. An example of his stature as a churchman during the two hundred years after his death can be seen in the hot exchange which resulted when Thomas Phillips cited him as an authority for the toleration of Roman Catholics (No. 396). This generated a book of contradiction by Ridley and one other response (Nos. 398 and 328). And although they are not included in this bibliography because they are only brief passing mentions of Taylor, such authors as Alexander Pope (*Moral Essays,* Ep. II), Charles Dickens (*Our Mutual Friend*), Nathaniel Hawthorne ("Egotism; or the Bosom Serpent"), George Eliot (*Middlemarch*), Thomas Hardy (*Tess of the D'Urbervilles*), and Christopher Fry (*A Phoenix Too Frequent*) made reference to Taylor, his works, and the fashion of reading his works.

In part the neglect of Taylor stems from the increasing secularization of the English-speaking world from the eighteenth century onward and in part from the gradual specialization of scholarly endeavors which separated the study of literature from the study of divinity—the areas of Taylor's greatest claims to fame. However, in the last few decades there has been an increasing interest in prose style, especially the prose styles of the seventeenth century, and this has generated a renewed interest in Taylor and his works. For example, of the 503 items in this bibliography not quite one-fifth appeared in the eighteenth century and, as I have noted above, most of these were editions of, or selections from, Taylor's works. However, by the end of the eighteenth century the English Romantics, especially Samuel Taylor Coleridge, had begun to show an interest in the sixteenth and seventeenth centuries, and with the Oxford Movement and its members' interests in the Caroline divines, the study of Taylor and comments about him increased rapidly. The period from 1790 to 1899 accounts for approximately one-half of the entries in this bibliography. All the collected editions of Taylor's works (Section I.C.) appeared between 1807 and 1870 and students of Taylor, for good or ill, must still rely heavily on the work of Heber and Eden (Nos. 178 and 186) as the standard editions. One final statistic in this regard: of the 187 items in Sections I.A.-C. only 29 appeared between 1860 and 1899 and only 22 from 1900 to 1976, or rather, 136 of 187 editions of various of Taylor's works, individual, collected, or abridged, have not been produced during any part of the period governed by modern textual criticism. This alone would argue persuasively that one of the areas of study that this bibliography shows to be neglected is textual criticism.

The division of Section II of this bibliography into subsections A (Biographical Studies), B (Theological Studies), and C (Literary Studies and General Studies) roughly approximates the primary foci of interest in Taylor over two and three-quarters centuries. As my annotations indicate, much Taylorian biography borders on, or lapses entirely into, hagiography. This was certainly true of the early biographies, for their prime concern was with Taylor as the "typical" Anglican or as the pious and reverend Bishop. Although there were some early exceptions—Willmott (1847; No. 323) and Heber (1824; No. 281)—the standard life is that of C.J. Stranks (1952; No. 313). The remainder of biographical study is scattered over journal articles, notes, and references in the works of others. Even Taylor's correspondence is essentially uncollected, and although Paul Elmen and I are in the process of preparing a collected edition, currently scholars must search through many and often scarce publications to piece together Taylor's life from Taylor's own words and those of his correspondents.

Much bibliographical work has been done, particularly the long and important researches of Robert Gathorne-Hardy (Nos. 270–276), but even here there has been sufficient additional information unearthed since the publication of the descriptive bibliography in 1971 to indicate that there will soon be a need for a major revision of this work.

Theological studies have primarily been concerned with five

topics: Taylor's doctrine of Original Sin, his contributions to liturgy, religious toleration, casuistry, and devotional literature. Of the nearly one hundred items in Section II.B. of the bibliography, about one-quarter are concerned, in various ways, with Taylor's views on religious toleration. Most authors are either utterly scornful of Taylor's work, seeing it as a case of special pleading easily thrown off after the Restoration, or they venerate Taylor's work as an early argument for religious freedom, often drawing parallels with the works of Hales, Chillingworth, and Milton in his *Areopagitica*. Needless to say, the question is far more complex than this.

Another one-quarter of the theological studies is nearly evenly divided between Taylor's liturgical contributions to Anglicanism and his founding, or re-founding, of English casuistry. The former area of interest is primarily focused on Taylor's various substitutes for the Book of Common Prayer during the Commonwealth period and on his liturgical work as a bishop after the Restoration. The latter area is concerned almost entirely with one work, *Ductor Dubitantium*, and with Taylor's provision of Anglicanism with a manual of casuistry which is a Protestant alternative to Roman Catholic manuals.

Surprisingly, only eight items are specifically concerned with Taylor as a writer of devotional works, even though it is a popular notion that his fame rests almost entirely on his works of this kind. What one discovers, however, is that much lip service is paid to his devotions, the other editions of *Holy Living* and *Holy Dying* since 1650–51 indicating a popular demand for these two works, but that very little serious study has been devoted to the theology and structure of this aspect of Taylor's corpus. However, the style of these works has been heavily studied, those items appearing in Section II.C.

Finally, four items (Nos. 334, 346, 356, and 372) specifically deal with Taylor's teachings on Original Sin. All find fault with Taylor, the latter two offering explanations about why Taylor held the views he did, the former two merely branding him as unorthodox, perhaps heretical; some comment on this point is also made in literary items in Section II.C.

One of the most important subjects of Taylor studies since

1700 has been his style. Of the nearly eighty items in the Literary Section of this bibliography twenty-nine are concerned with that subject, with varying degrees of precision and elaboration. Many of the items, like those of Coleridge (Nos. 435–440), are very general comments about his style; some rely on epithet and catch phrase, such as James Russell Lowell's calling Taylor "a kind of Spenser in a cassock" (No. 470). However, some make a more solid contribution to the study of his style, notably Nos. 428, 451, 452, 464, 477, 496, and 500.

For an author as popular as Taylor was, it is not surprising that about a quarter of the items in the Literary and General Section of this bibliography deal either with other authors' borrowings from him or with his borrowings from earlier writers, particularly Montaigne.

In summary, although Taylor's reputation with the general reading public has sadly waned during the last hundred years, as is shown by the rapid slow-down in the publication of editions of his works, this has been partly offset by a rise in interest in him in the world of scholarship since the mid-nineteenth century. In this regard Taylor is not unlike many other authors of this period, including Milton and only excepting Shakespeare. It is to be hoped that scholarly interest will eventually produce a synthesis which will not only give us new and better ways to read and understand him, but which will also restore him to his proper place among the classic writers of English prose and "early fathers" of Anglicanism.

•   •   •

I have attempted to make this checklist as complete as possible, within the limits stated below, but because of Taylor's popularity among so many audiences, certainly some reprints of sermons and articles concerning him will have been overlooked, and I would be grateful to have them called to my attention.

The entries for individual editions of Taylor's works, and abridgments and selections from one work (Sections I.A. and I.B.), are arranged alphabetically by title and chronologically within each title group. Those parts of a single work which have, over the years, lived a literary and bibliographical life of their own (e.g., Nos. 132–142, "A Moral Demonstration," which is Chapter IV of *Ductor Dubitantium*) are treated apart from the main work, and are so indicated in their title headings. The collected editions (Section I.C.) and abridgments and selections from two or more works (Section I.D.) are arranged chronologically. I have made no attempt to indicate the contents of books in the latter classes, since this is either evident from their titles or is so diverse that this bibliographical checklist would become hopelessly burdened with annotations. I have included several works of disputed authorship (e.g., Nos. 002–013) and have annotated each entry of this kind accordingly. I have selectively included reprintings, but I have attempted to exclude reissues or new impressions. For most items in sections I.A.–I.D. a limited list of locations of copies is provided. If no notation is given the location is the British Library; if any locations do appear, the British Library is included only if specifically mentioned. If I have been unable to find a location, that is also noted by the addition of "N.C." for "no copy observed."

The three sections of studies (II.A.–II.C.) are arranged alphabetically, and are annotated. In some cases, placing a work in a particular section has been, of necessity, arbitrary, and I have included all bibliographical and non-theological background studies in the Biography section. I have not included general reference works, general literary histories either of English literature or specifically of the seventeenth century, and similar general works unless I have decided that their contribution is significant. Some reprints have been listed because of their historical importance, such as the first American edition of Heber's *Life* (No. 282), but normally they have not been recorded. In annotating entries I have attempted to describe briefly the contents of the item and I have not felt it inappropriate to offer my judgment about the item's quality or usefulness. Some items are fully explained by their titles, and these are merely annotated with "S.E." for "self-explanatory." In a few instances circumstances beyond my control made it impossible for me to obtain a copy of the item and, assuming discretion to be the better part of valor, I have not tried to guess at annotations from secondary sources. These items are marked with "N.C." for "no copy observed." The Index of Authors lists all authors and editors of books and articles, and the Index of Works lists entries in Sections II.A.–C. which treat specific works by Taylor.

Finally, I would like to thank Messrs. Samuel T. Huang, William R. DuBois, and Anthony Bliss of the Northern Illinois University Library, the staffs of the Northern Illinois University Libraries, the Kansas State University Library, the British Library, the Newberry Library, and the Library of Trinity College, Dublin, for their special assistance in locating and acquiring materials. I also would like to indicate the deep debt I owe to my late friend, Mr. Robert Gathorne-Hardy, for the use of the results of his long researches on Taylor to double-check some of my information. I would also like to thank the Department of English of Northern Illinois University for its assistance in the preparation of the manuscript, and Professors Charles A. Pennel, Fred H. Higginson, and Dr. Philip R. Rider for their help and advice.

William P. Williams
Northern Illinois University
DeKalb

ABBREVIATIONS

DD	*Ductor Dubitantium*
GE	*Great Exemplar*
HD	*Holy Dying*
HL	*Holy Living*
LP	*Liberty of Prophesying*
UN	*Unum Necessarium*

AN&Q	*American Notes and Queries*
DA	*Dissertation Abstracts*
HLQ	*Huntington Library Quarterly*
McNamee	McNamee, Lawrence F. *Dissertations in English and American Literature: Theses Accepted by American, British and German Universities, 1865–1964.* New York, 1968.
N&Q	*Notes & Queries*
TLS	*Times Literary Supplement*

A.A.S.	American Antiquarian Soc., Worcester, Mass.
B.L.	British Library
Bod.	Bodleian Library
Cinc.	University of Cincinnati Library
Col.	Columbia University Library
I.U.	University of Illinois Library
K.S.U.	Kansas State University Library
K.U.	Kansas University Library
L.C.	Library of Congress
N.C.	No copy observed, item verified from secondary sources.
N.I.U.	Northern Illinois University Library
N.L.	Newberry Library
N.Y.	New York Public Library
S.E.	Self-explanatory
W.	William P. Williams

THE WORKS
(POST 1700)

I. A. INDIVIDUAL WORKS

ACADEMIA COELESTIS; OR THE HEAVENLY UNIVERSITY
[Sermon at Trinity College, Dublin].

001 London, 1819.

CONTEMPLATIONS OF THE STATE OF MAN [Doubtful
authorship].

002 London, 1702.

003 London, 1707.

004 London, 1717.

005 London, 1718.

006 Boston, 1721. [N.C.].

007 London, 1724; Yng Nghaer-lleon, [1740?]. [Welsh
translation, published as Ystyriaethu o Gyflwr Dyn
yn y bywyd hwn ac yn yr hwn sy i ddyfod, trans.
Griffith Wynn]. [B.L., L.C.].

008 London, 1726. [N. C.].

009 London, 1734.

010 Ed. John Nelson Goulty. London, 1815.

011 Ed. T. Griffith and G. Anwyl. Merthyr Tydvil,
1825. [Welsh translation, published as Ystyriaethu
o Gyflwr Dyn yn y bywyd hwn ac yn yr
hwn sy i ddyfod].

012 London, 1845.

013 London, 1847. [Rpt. of No. 012].

CHRISTIAN SIMPLICITY [Sermon on Matt. 10.16].

014 Edinburgh (Bishops' Tracts, no. 10), 1858.

A DISCOURSE OF BAPTISM

015 London, 1754. [N.C.].

016 in Christian Institutes, 4 vols., ed. Christopher
     Wordsworth. London, 1837 (2: 47-105). [B.L.,
     I.U.].

A DISCOURSE OF FRIENDSHIP

017 London, 1920.

A DISSUASIVE FROM POPERY

018 in Enchiridion Theologicum Anti-Romanum, 3 vols.,
     ed. E. Cardwell. Oxford University Press, 1836 (1: 1-477).
     [B.L., Cinc.].

DOOMS-DAY BOOK; OR, CHRIST'S ADVENT TO JUDGMENT
     [Sermon on 2 Cor. 5.10].

019 in The World's Great Sermons, 10 vols., ed. G.
     Kleiser and L. O. Brastow. New York, 1908 (2:
     30-56). [N.I.U.].

FIDES FORMATA [Sermon on James 2.24].

020 Ed. R. Nelson. London, 1827; Bath,
     1827. [Copy of Bath edition in Bod.].

THE FOOLISH EXCHANGE [Sermon on Matt. 16.26].

021 in History and Repository of Pulpit Eloquence,
     2 vols., ed. H. C. Fish. New York, 1857 (1:
     556-581). [B.L., I.U.].

022   in The Great Sermons of Great Preachers.   London:
      Cassell, Petter, and Calpin, 1858.   [N.C.].

FUNERAL SERMON FOR BRAMHALL

023   in The Works of John Bramhall.   5 vols.   Oxford,
      1842 (1: xxxix-lxxvi). [reprinted from Heber's
      edition, No. 178].

THE GOLDEN GROVE

024   London, 1703.

025   London, 1713.

026   London, 1719.   [W.].

027   London, 1735.

028   London, 1811.   [Bod.].

029   London, 1822.

030   Oxford, 1836.   [Bod.].

031   Oxford, 1839.   [Bod.].

032   Oxford, 1843.   [Bod.].

033   Oxford, 1868.   [Bod.].

THE GREAT EXEMPLAR, OR THE HISTORY OF THE LIFE AND
DEATH OF THE EVER BLESSED JESUS CHRIST

034   in Antiquitates Christianae, 2 vols.   London,
      1702-1703 (vol. 1).

035   London, 1742.

036 Exeter, N. H., 1794. [A.A.S.].

037 Newburyport, Mass., 1796. [B.L., N.Y.].

038 Greenfield, Mass., 1796. [B.L., L.C., N.Y.].

039 2 vols. London, 1811.

040 in The Sacred Classics, 30 vols., ed. R.
Cattermole and H. Stebbing. London, 1835 (vols.
22-24). [B.L., N.L.].

041 Ed. Robert Philip. London, 1836. [Bod.].

042 3 vols. London (Pickering edition), 1849. [B.L.,
L.C., W.].

043 Ed. T. A. Buckley. London, 1851.

044 New York, 1859. [L.C.].

GUNPOWDER SERMON

045 New York, 1971. [Facs. of the 1638 edition, STC
23724].

HEAVEN

046 Heaven, a hymn by J. Taylor. Sung at the Com-
memoration Service, June 22, 1898, at the Celebra-
tion of the 550th Anniversary of the Foundation of
the College [Gonville & Caius]. Composed by
Charles Wood. The Caian, 3 (1898): 145.

HOLY LIVING and HOLY DYING

[Here and in the section of abridgments, Holy Living
and Holy Dying are first treated in their
combined appearances and then in their separate
appearances].

047 London, 1700.

048 Llundain [London], 1701. [Welsh translation published as Rheol buchedd sanctaidd yn dangos y moddion a'r arrfeu i ynnill pob gras, trans. E. Wynne].

049 London, 1703.

050 London, 1706.

051 London, 1710.

052 London, 1715. [W.].

053 London, 1719.

054 London, 1727. [W.].

055 London, 1739.

056 in A Christian Library, 50 vols., ed. John Wesley. Bristol, 1749-1755 (vol. 9).

057 2 vols., ed. T. Thirlwall. London, 1810-1812. [W.].

058 2 vols. London and Glasgow, 1820.

059 with a memoir of the author's life. London, 1824. [W.].

060 With a Life of the Author, 2 vols., ed. "J." Edinburgh, 1826. [W.].

061 Together with Prayers. London, 1839?. [N.C.].

062 London (Bohn's Standard Library), 1846.

063 2 vols. Oxford, 1857.

064 London, 1859. [Bod].

065   2 vols. London, 1868.

066   2 vols. London, 1869. [Rpt. of 059].

067   Ed. F. A. Malleson. London, 1879.

068   London, 1882. [N.C.].

069   Ed. "E. A." London, 1885. [N.C.].

070   London (Ancient and Modern Library of Theological
      Literature), 1887.

071   in Cassell's National Library, 209 vols., ed.
      Henry Morley. London, 1888-1889 (vols. 153-
      154; 167-168).

072   Ed. F. A. Malleson. London, 1894. [New ed., see
      No. 067].

073   London (Sir John Lubbock's 100 Books, no. 74),
      1891.

074   London (Bell edition), 1897. [B.L., L.C.]; rpt.
      London, 1913. [W.].

075   Caerdydd [Cardiff], 1928. [Facs. of 048].

                    HOLY DYING

076   Yarmouth, 1814. [Bod.].

077   With a memoir of the author. London, 1827.
      [Bod.].

078   London (Pickering edition), 1845. [N.C.].

079   New York, 1859. [B.L., W.].

080   London, 1878.

                         8

081 Ed. Correlli(?). London, 1885; 1889. [Bod.].

HOLY LIVING

082 London, 1703.

083 London, 1710.

084 London, 1727. [W.].

085 Ed. Thomas Thirlwall. London, 1807.

086 Yarmouth, 1813. [Bod.].

087 Ed. Thomas Thirlwall. Boston, 1820. [L.C., N.L.].

088 London (Pickering edition), 1848.

089 Philadelphia, 1872. [B.L., W.].

090 London, 1879.

091 Oxford, 1880. [Bod.].

092 London, 1885; 1886. [Bod.].

093 London (Ancient and Modern Library of Theology and Literature, no. 7), 1888? [W.].

094 London (Bagster's Christian Classics), 1894.

095 2 vols., ed. A. R. Waller. London (Temple Classics), 1900.

096 London (Everyman's Library), 1930. [B.L., L.C.].

IN HONOUR OF SAINT JOHN

097 McClure's Magazine, 34 (1910): 243. [Poem from "Festival Hymns"].

098 London, 1702. [B.L., K.S.U., W.].

099 London, 1709. [B.L., K.U.].

100 London, 1817.

101 in The Sacred Classics, 30 vols., ed. R.
Cattermole and H. Stebbing. London, 1835 (vol.
1). [B.L., N.L.].

102 Menston, Yorkshire, 1971. [Facs. of the 1647
edition, Wing T400].

THE MARRIAGE RING [Sermon on Eph. 5.32-33].

103 London, 1840. [Bod.].

104 London, 1850. [Bod.].

105 in The Manual of Matrimony. London, 1854.
[N.C.].

106 London, 1863.

107 Ed. F. A. Kerr. London, 1883.

108 Ed. F. B. Money Coutts. Cambridge, 1883; London,
1883; 1884; Oxford, 1892. [Rpt. from 1673
Eniautos, Wing T332]. [Bod.].

109 in Masterpieces of Oratory, 4 vols., ed. Richard
Garnett. New York, 1900 (1: 144-174). [K.S.U.].

110 Glasgow (Gowan's International Library), 1906.

111 Ed. Francis B. Money Coutts. New York , 1907.
[Rpt. of 1673 Eniautos, Wing T332, with frontis.
of Perugino's 'Marriage of the Virgin'; cf.
098].

112 in Famous Sermons by English Preachers, ed.
Douglas Macleane. London, 1911 (pp. 83-96).
[N.L.].

113 Illus. Denis Tegetmeier. Abergavenny, 1928.
[Appears under the title The Mysteriousness of
Marriage]. [B.L., L.C.].

114 in Selected English Sermons, ed. H. H. Henson.
Oxford (World's Classics), 1939 (pp. 125-163).
[B.L., L.C.].

ON THE REVERENCE DUE TO THE ALTAR

115 Now first printed from the original manuscript,
ed. J. Barrow. Oxford, 1848.

116 Ed. Vernon Staley. Oxford, 1899.

THE PSALTER OF DAVID

117 London, 1702.

118 London, 1724. [Bod.].

119 London, 1826.

120 London, 1832.

THE REAL PRESENCE, OR A DISCOURSE ON THE LORD'S SUPPER

121 London, 1792.

122 in Enchiridion Theologicum Anti-Romanum, 3 vols.,
ed. E. Cardwell. Oxford, 1836 (1: 479-665).
[B.L., Cinc.].

123 in Enchiridion Theologicum, 5 vols., ed. J. Randolph.
London, 1792 (vol. 2). [N.C.].

124 in Clergyman's Instructor. Oxford, 1807; 1824
(pp. 97-112). [I.U.].

ARTIFICIAL HANDSOMENESS [Doubtful authorship].

125 Several Letters Between Two Ladies. London, 1701.

TWO LETTERS TO A LADY

126 in Christian Institutes, 4 vols., ed. Christopher
Wordsworth. London, 1837 (4: 249-274). [B.L.,
I.U.].

UNUM NECESSARIUM

127 London, 1705.

128 London, 1711.

129 London, 1712.

THE WORTHY COMMUNICANT

130 London, 1701.

131 London, 1853.

I. B. ABRIDGMENTS OF INDIVIDUAL WORKS

A MORAL DEMONSTRATION: Chapter IV of DUCTOR
DUBITANTIUM

132 London, 1775.

133 London, 1776.

134 in The Scholar Armed, 2 vols., ed. William Jones.
London, 1795 (2: 353-384). [B.L., N.L.].

135 in The Scholar Armed, 2 vols., ed. William Jones.
London, 1800 (2: 299-324). [B.L., N.L., Col.].

136 Abr. T. Waite. London, 1818.

137 Ed. C. Girdlestone. London, 1831. [Bod.].

138 London (SPCK tract, no. 1), 1836.

139 in The Christian Armed, ed. Thomas Jackson.
London, 1837 (pp. 163-229). [B.L., N.L.].

140 in Christian Institutes, 4 vols., ed. Christopher
Wordsworth. London, 1837 (1: 57-85). [B.L.,
I.U.].

141 in Theological Tracts, 3 vols., ed. J. Brown.
London, 1853 (vol. 2).

142 Abr. Thomas Greene. Chichester, 1879.

DUCTOR DUBITANTIUM

143 2 vols., abr. R. Barcroft; preface by R. Fiddes.
London, 1725.

144 The Jewish Sabbath and the Lord's Day, ed. Sir
Richard Musgrove. London, 1843. [Bod.].

THE FLESH AND THE SPIRIT [Sermon on Matt. 26.41].

145 How to Cure an Evil Nature. Decision, (May, 1972): 7.

146 Guide to the Penitent from the Golden Grove.
London, 1852. [Bod.].

THE GREAT EXEMPLAR, OR THE HISTORY OF THE LIFE
AND DEATH OF THE EVER BLESSED JESUS CHRIST

147 London, ca. 1730. [N.I.U.].

148 London, 1758.

149 Greenfield, Mass., 1796.

150 Portsmouth, R. I., 1796. [See No. 149]. [B.L.,
L.C.].

151 Lives of the Evangelists. Leominster, Mass.,
1797. [N.C.].

152 Abr. W. N. Darnell. London, 1818.

153 Abr. A[rthur] M[ozley]. London, 1849.

154 The Prayers Contained in the Life of Christ
by Bishop Jeremy Taylor. London, 1854.

155 London, 1882.

156 The Advent Season: Devotional Readings from
Bishop Taylor's Life of Christ, ed. J. E. Kempe.
London, 1899. [Bod.].

157 The Holy Week: Devotional Readings from
Bishop Taylor's Life of Christ, ed. J. E. Kempe.
London (CKS), 1899.

158 Bishop Taylor's The Great Exemplar, Selections
from the Revised Edition of the Rev.
Robert Philip, 1836. Cambridge, 1910. [See No. 041].

14

HOLY LIVING and HOLY DYING

159 Manual of Piety Extracted from the Holy
Living and Dying, ed. R. Fellowes. London, 1807.

160 Abr. W. H. Hale. London, 1838.

161 A Little Scroll of Counsels and Cautions:
Extracted from the Holy Living and Dying. London,
1850. [N.C.].

HOLY DYING

162 The Sick Man's Guide, ed. W. H. Hale. London,
1838.

163 Ed. Thomas Kepler. New York, 1952. [B.L., L.C.].

HOLY LIVING

164 Bishop Taylor's Introduction to a Holy
Life. London (SPCK), 1833.

165 Prayers and Thanksgivings from Holy Living.
London, 1867.

166 London (SPCK), 1940.

167 Ed. Thomas Kepler. New York, 1956. [B.L., L.C.].

168 Abr. Anne Lamb; foreword, Henry Chadwick. Ramford,
Essex, 1970.

HOUSE OF FEASTING

169 in Sermons and Society, ed. Paul A. Welsby. London,
1970 (pp. 123-126). [W.].

15

170 A Scheme of Plea, for and Against the
Baptizing of Infants. London, 1717. [Bod.].

171 A Discourse on Freedom of Thinking in
Matters of Religion. Oxford, 1763. [Bod.].

172 The Baptists Justified, ed. and intro. W.
Anderson. London, 1818. [LP,
Chapter 18].

MARRIAGE RING

173 in Master Sermons Through the Ages, ed. W. A.
Sadler, Jr. New York, 1963 (pp. 110-117). [L.C., N.I.U.].

UNUM NECESSARIUM

174 Doctrine of Repentance, abr. W. H. Hale. London,
1836.

VIA INTELLIGENTIAE

175 Stray Leaves: Extracts from Via
Intelligentiae. Calcutta, 1850.

THE WORTHY COMMUNICANT

176 A Discourse of the Holy Sacrament Abridged
from The Worthy Communicant, by a Member of
the Established Church. Bath, 1822.

I. C. COLLECTED EDITIONS

177 Discourses on Various Subjects, 3 vols. London,
1807; Boston, 1816. [Sermons].

178 The Whole Works, with a Life of the
Author, 15 vols., ed. Reginald Heber. London, 1822;
1828.

179 A Course of Sermons, 2 vols. London, 1826.
[Bod.].

180 The Works, with Some Account of His Life,
5 vols., ed. T. S. Hughes. London, 1831.

181 Select Sermons. The Sacred Classics, 30 vols.,
ed. R. Cattermole and H. Stebbing. London, 1834
(vol. 7). [Miracles of Divine Mercy, pp. 1-70; Of
the Spirit of Grace, pp. 71-114; The
Deceitfulness of the Heart, pp. 115-154; The
Marriage Ring, pp. 155-192; The Righteousness
Evangelical, pp. 193-224; The Christian's
Conquest over the Body of Sin, pp. 225-255; Fides
Formata, pp. 256-289; Faith and Patience of the
Saints, pp.z290-357].

182 The Golden Grove and The Worthy Communicant. In
John Fleetwood, The Life of . . . Christ. London, 1837
(pp. 665-891). [Taylor's two works are appended to
Fleetwood's work] [B.L., W.].

183 The Practical Works, with a Sketch of the
Life and Times of the Author, 8 vols., ed. George
Croly. London, 1838.

184 Selected Works. Illustrations of the Liturgy, 3
vols., ed. J. Brogden. London, 1842.

[Christian's Conquest, Funeral Sermon for Lady
Carbery, The Marriage Ring, Miracles of
Divine Mercy, The Righteousness Evangelical,
Sermon on James 2.24, Sermon on Luke 12.
42-43, Via Intelligentiae, On the Duty
of Nursing Children].

185 The Whole Works, with an Essay Biographical
and Critical, 3 vols. London, 1844 and 1880.

186 The Whole Works, with a life of the Author,
10 vols., ed. Reginald Heber; revised and corrected
by C. P. Eden. London, 1847-1852.

187 The Poems and Verse Translations, ed. A. B.
Grosart. London (Fuller's Worthies Library,
vol. 1), 1870.

17

I. D. COLLECTIONS OF SELECTED PORTIONS OF TAYLOR'S
WORKS

188 Cydymaith yr Eglwyswr yn ymweled a'r claf
[A Clergyman's Companion]. London, 1700.

189 Occasional Prayers. The Devout Christian's
Companion. London, 1707; 1708; 1722. [N.C.].

190 Devout Christian's Companion. London, 1710. [N.C.].

191 The Clergyman's Companion for Visiting the
Sick. London, 1723.

192 The Complete Manual of Family and Private
Devotions. Manchester, 1741. [Collected from
several bishops]. [N.C.].

193 Sacred Annals: of the Life of Christ. London, 1776.
[N.C.].

194 A Selection of Prayers from Jeremy Taylor.
Dorchester, 1800.

195 Selections from the Works of Taylor, . . ., ed.
Basil Montagu. London, 1805 (pp. 1-119). London,
1807; 1829; 1833; 1835; 1839; 1896. [Appeared in the
1896 edition under the title Thoughts of Divines and
Philosophers as part of the Temple Classics
series].

196 Prayers Selected from the Several Writings
of Jeremy Taylor, ed. S. Clapham. London, 1810; 1816;
1826; 1843.

197 Fifteen Sermons Taken from the Discourses
of Jeremy Taylor, to which are Added Three
Sermons Preached by D. Lyons. London, 1818. [N.C.].

198 Select British Divines, 28 vols., ed. C. Bradley.
London, 1821 (vols. 20-21).

199 A Few Useful Hints in Determining What is
Called Catholic Emancipation, Collected from
the Works of Jeremy Taylor. London, 1826.

200 A Few Forms of Morning and Evening Prayer
from the Works of Jeremy Taylor, ed. S. Corbett.
London, 1827.

201 A Preparation for the Sacrament Selected
from Jeremy Taylor. London, 1829; 1864.

202 Summaries of the Sermons of the Most
Eminent Divines, ed. T. S. Hughes. London, 1834.

203 Selections from the Works of Jeremy Taylor. A
Collection of Essays and Tracts, 6 vols., ed.
Jared Sparks. London, 1838 (vol. 6). [N.C.].

204 The Churchman's Companion with Selections
from Bishop Jeremy Taylor. London, 1840. [N.C.].

205 Prayers at the Communion by Bishop Taylor,
ed. T. Stephen. London, 1841.

206 Fragments on the Lord's Supper, from the
Works of Bishop Jeremy Taylor. London, 1842.

207 Pictures of Religion in a Selection from
Taylor. London, 1842.

208 The Beauties of Jeremy Taylor, ed. "B. S., Esq."
London, 1845.

209 Half Hours with the Best Authors. 4 vols.,
ed. Charles Knight. London, 1847-1848 (various editions
thereafter) (1: 185-193; 2: 52-55, 313-315).

210 Readings for Lent from the Writings of
Taylor, ed. Miss E. M. Sewell. London, 1851.

211 Prayer for the Army and Navy in Time
of War. Oxford, 1854. [N.C.].

212 A Book of Family Prayer Chiefly from the
Devotions of Taylor, ed. G. W. Cox. London, 1862; 1876.

213 Preparation for the Holy Communion. London, 1864.
[Bod.].

214 Selections from the Works of Jeremy Taylor.
Boston, 1865. [L.C.].

215 Godly Fear: Selections from Taylor. Edinburgh,
1869; London, 1875.

216 Jeremy Taylor's Prayers for a Household.
London, 1873.

217 Selections from the Works of . . . Jeremy
Taylor. . . ., ed. Henry Jenkins. London, 1876.

218 Jeremy Taylor: Brief Passages from His
Writings. London (Church Lamps series), 1882.

219 Saintly Words: Being Devout Thoughts from
Augustine . . . and Jeremy Taylor. London, 1883.
[N.C.].

220 Holy Living: A Year-Book of Thoughts from
Taylor, ed. F. W. Farrar. London, 1884; 1885.

221 Selections from Taylor, with Some Account
of the Author and His Writings. London, 1884.

222 Jeremy Taylor's Golden Sayings, ed. J. Dennis.
London, 1893.

223 The Presence of God: Selections from the
Devotional Works of Jeremy Taylor, ed. F. E.
Clark. Boston, 1898. [L.C.].

224 The Advent Season: Devotions from Taylor,
ed. J. E. Kempe. London (CKS), 1899.

225 Women's Prayers: Collected from Taylor, ed. "H.
S." Oxford, 1899.

226 Selections from Taylor. London, 1905.

227 Jeremy Taylor: A Selection from His Works,
   ed. Martin Armstrong. Waltham Saint Lawrence (Golden
   Cockerel Press), 1923. [B.L., L.C., K.S.U.].

228 The Golden Grove: Selected Passages from Taylor
   with a Bibliography of the Works . . . by
   Robert Gathorne-Hardy, ed. Logan Pearsall Smith.
   Oxford, 1930. [B.L., L.C., K.S.U.].

229 The House of Understanding: Selections from
   Taylor, ed. Margaret Gest. Philadelphia, 1954.
   [B.L., L.C., K.S.U.].

230 The Wisdom of Jeremy Taylor, ed. Richard Tatlock.
   London, 1954.

231 Wings of An Eagle, An Anthology of Caroline
   Preachers, ed. G. Lacey May. London, 1955.

232 In God's Name, ed. John Chandos. London, 1971
   (pp. 481-511).

233 The English Sermon, 2 vols., ed. C. H. Sisson.
   London, 1976.

THE STUDIES

II. A. BIOGRAPHICAL STUDIES

234 "Holy Living." The Christian Observer, 6
(1807): 733-738.

A brief general review of Taylor and this work.

235 (Anon.). "Jeremy Taylor." Quarterly Review, 131
(1871): 60-77.

A review of Nos. 186 and 323 which prints a letter by
Taylor, 17 April 1658, and extracts from many others
which were all in the possession of Mr. Murray.

236 (Anon.). Jeremy Taylor: His Life. London (Church
of England Biographies, 1st Series), 1871.

A popular general biography which makes no new
contributions to Taylor's biography.

237 (Anon.). Life of Jeremy Taylor. London: CKS,
1865.

A popular biography of Taylor not based on any
new facts or research.

238 (Anon.). "Sketches and Anecdotes of Worthies of
the English Church." Sharpe's London Magazine, 13
(1850): 350-360.

A popular biography of Taylor with concentration on
the "high spots" of his career as a clergyman.

239 Adair, Patrick. True Narrative of the Rise of the
Presbyterian Church in Ireland. Belfast: W. D. Killen,
1866 (passim).

A rather biased view of Taylor's episcopal conduct
in Ireland, though still one of the standard sources
for biographical information.

240 Atkinson, Edward Dupre. An Ulster Parish.
Dublin: Hodges, Figgis & Co. Ltd., 1898 (p. 28).

Briefly mentions Taylor in connection with his episcopal
duties in Ulster.

241 Ball, Johnson. William Caslon. Kineton: Roundwood
Press, 1973 (pp. 297, plates 26 and 27).

Discusses the engraved title-page of the 1657 GE and
reproduces both it and the letterpress title-page.

242 Bigger, Francis Joseph, and William J. Fennell.
"The Middle Church of Ballinderry and Bishop Jeremy
Taylor." Ulster Journal of Archaeology, 3 n.s. (1896):
13-22, 277.

Describes the ruins of the church which Taylor
first knew and the church built here by him, as well
as the communion table, chalice, and other fittings
of the latter church; also points out that the Portmore,
Killultagh of Taylor's letters and dedications is
this place. Numerous illustrations and scale drawings.

243 Birch, Thomas. The Life of Dr. John Tillotson.
London: J. & R. Tonson, 1752 (pp. 19-20).

Includes Taylor in a list of the distinguished preachers
and churchmen from the time of Edward VI to the death
of James I, saying that Taylor is "the Barrow of an
earlier date."

244 Bone, Gavin. "Jeremy Taylor and Elizabeth
Grymeston." The Library, 4th series, 15 (1934):
247-248.

A brief note demonstrating the similarity of the
silkworm simile in Grymeston and Taylor's XXVIII
Sermons.

245 Bonney, Henry Kaye. Life of Bishop Jeremy Taylor.
London: T. Cadell and W. Davies, 1815.

One of the earliest biographies of Taylor, treating
Taylor's life in rather strict chronological terms;
each chapter is subtitled with the period of years
covered. Bonney relies heavily on Rust's funeral
sermon for his information and very little original
research is in evidence.

246 Bramhall, John. Works, 5 vols., ed. A. W. Haddan.
Oxford: J. H. Parker, 1842-1845 (1: xii, xli-lxxvi).

Brief information of Taylor's early episcopal work
in Ireland, especially as it is concerned with his
dealings with Archbishop Bramhall.

247 Brokesby, Francis. The Life of Mr. Dodwell with
    an Account of His Works. London: G. James for R. Smith,
    1715.

    N.C.

248 Brown, John Taylor. "Bibliomania." Odds and Ends.
    No. 19. Edinburgh: Edmonston & Douglas, 1867 (pp. 4,
    9-11, 13).

    A discussion of textual corruption in the works of
    seventeenth-century writers. In the case of Taylor
    the example is of "lazars" corrupted to "Lazarus" in
    HD, Ch. I, sect. 3, SS 2,3.

249 Brown, William James. Jeremy Taylor. London:
    Macmillan (English Theologians series), 1925.

    Brief biography followed by a description and
    analysis of his writings; both a popular and learned
    work clearly aimed at a middle audience.

250 Brown, William James. "Jeremy Taylor's Sermons."
    TLS, January 11, 1952, p. 25.

    A brief list and description of the summaries of
    nine Taylor sermons made by John Evelyn after hearing
    them, as preserved in the Evelyn manuscripts then on
    loan to Christ Church, Oxford.

251 'Caius Man, A.' "Comments on the Biography of Jeremy
    Taylor." Gentleman's Magazine, 53 (1855): 376-380.

    As a supplement to Heber and Willmott's biographies
    (Nos. 281 and 323), discusses Taylor's birthplace and
    prints a modern picture of the "Wrestlers' Inn,"
    Cambridge, the traditional birthplace, but suggests
    the real place may be the "Black Bear" and presents
    further information about his exact date of birth.
    The writer also provides new details about Taylor's
    career at Cambridge, his first marriage, and his
    successor at Uppingham.

252 Carey, Henry. Memorials of the Civil War, 2 vols.
    London, 1842 (2: 75-100).

    Prints a long letter from Taylor to Dr. Richard
    Bayly, Vigils of Christmas 1648, on the subject
    of the alienation of church lands.

253 Carmody, W. P. Lisburn Cathedral and Its Past
Rectors. Belfast: R. Carswell, 1926.

S.E.

254 Carte, Thomas. A History of James, Duke of
Ormonde, 3 vols. London: P. Knapton, 1736 (2: 208-209).

Describes Taylor's appointments as Bishop of Down and as
Chancellor of Trinity College, Dublin, and indicates the
part Ormonde played in these events.

255 Conway Letters, ed. M. H. Nicolson. New Haven: Yale
University Press, 1930 (passim).

Discusses Taylor's relationship with the Conways
from Lord Conway becoming his "patron" in the
1650's until Taylor's death; reprints many letters
which mention Taylor written by various of Lady
Conway's correspondents.

256 Cooper, Anthony Ashley. Characteristics, 2 vols.,
ed. John M. Robertson; intro. by Stanley
Green. New York: E.P. Dutton & Co., 1900 (1: 67-68fn;
2: 180-181, 358-359).

Comments on private friendships citing Taylor's
Friendship as an authority; comments on martyrdom
citing Taylor's story of martyrs for and against
Savanarola in LP; and cites the same work concerning
sacred literature and the appropriate criticism
thereof.

257 Correspondence of the Family of Hatton, 2 vols.,
ed. Sir Edward Maunde Thompson. London: Camden Society,
1878 (1: 26-27).

Reprints one letter from Taylor to Lord Hatton, written
from Dublin, 23 November 1661.

258 Cotton, H. Fasti Ecclesiae Hibernicae, 5 vols.
London: J. H. Parker, 1848-1878 (passim, esp. vol. 3).

While providing a biographical record of the Irish
clergy this work naturally treats Taylor's diocese
and the clergy which he appointed, removed, and
governed.

259 Cropper, Margaret. Flame Touches Flame. London:
Longmans, Green, & Co., 1949 (pp. 103-154).

A brief, popular, and chatty biography of Taylor
relying heavily on received opinion and copious
quotation from Taylor's works and letters.

260 'Curious, Will.' [Untitled letter]. Gentleman's
Magazine, 53 (1783): 144.

Reports a local tradition that Taylor lived at
Maidley-Hall near Tamworth during the Civil War.

261 de Beer, E. S. "Jeremy Taylor" in 1655. N&Q, 17
(1936): 24-25.

Uses dates in John Evelyn's Diary to date more
accurately Taylor's letters during this year and
to more precisely determine his whereabouts and
activities.

262 Dixon, MacNeile. Trinity College, Dublin.
London, 1902 (pp. 52-53).

A very brief general discussion of Taylor's short
career as Chancellor and his proposed reforms.

263 Dugdale, William. The Life and Diary of Sir
William Dugdale, ed. William Hamper. London: Harding,
Lepard & Co., 1827 (pp. 250-251, 317).

Prints two letters from Taylor to Dugdale: 1 April 1651,
written from Golden Grove; 22 November 1656.

264 Duyckinck, G. L. Life of Bishop Jeremy Taylor.
New York: Gen. Protestant Episcopal Sunday School Union,
1860.

Popular life and writings biography of no scholarly
significance.

265 Evelyn, John. Diary, 6 vols., ed. E. S. de Beer.
Oxford: Oxford University Press, 1955 (passim).

Many references to Taylor and correspondence between
Evelyn and Taylor; of especial importance for the
period 1650-1661.

266 Evelyn, John. Memoirs, 1641-1706, 6 vols., ed.
William Bray. London: Colburn, 1818 (passim).

As in No. 265.

267 Ewart, Lavens. Handbook of the Diocese of Down.
Belfast, 1886 (passim).

S.E.

268 Farrar, F. W. "Jeremy Taylor." Masters of English
Theology, ed. Alfred Barry. London: Murray, 1877 (pp.
175-211).

A general biography of Taylor as churchman, theologian,
and preacher.

269 Fraser, William. Memorials of the Montgomeries, 2
vols. Edinburgh, 1859 (1: 313-314).

Prints Taylor's letter from Portmore to Hugh, 7th Earl
of Eglintoun, 7 December 1663, and also reproduces
Taylor's signature in facsimile.

270 Gathorne-Hardy, Robert, and William Proctor
Williams. A Bibliography of the Writings of
Jeremy Taylor to 1700, with a Section of
Tayloriana. DeKalb, Illinois: NIU Press, 1971.

A full descriptive bibliography of all editions to
1700, as well as supositious works, printings of
letters, and Tayloriana. Also reproduces a unique
portrait of Taylor.

271 Gathorne-Hardy, Robert. "Some Notes on the
Bibliography of Jeremy Taylor." The Library, 5th
series, 2 (1948): 233-249.

A progress report on his work on the bibliography of .
Taylor which eventually appeared as No. 270. He deals
with many points, particularly the variants of the
early editions of HL, the imprint of GE, and the
plates in the latter work.

272 Gathorne-Hardy, Robert. "The Bibliography of
Jeremy Taylor." The Library, 5th series, 3 (1948):
66.

As an addendum to No. 271, Gathorne-Hardy hypothesises
that the GE title-pages may indeed be twins rather
than simply variant.

273 Gathorne-Hardy, Robert. "Jeremy Taylor and 'Christian Consolations.'" TLS, April 20, 1951, p. 245.

Reports the discovery of a proof catalogue of Richard Royston's for 1678 which announces that Christian Consolations is by John Hackett. For further discussion of this disputed authorship question see No. 434.

274 Gathorne-Hardy, Robert. "Jeremy Taylor and Hatton's 'Psalter of David.'" TLS, February 18, 1955, p. 112.

An argument for attributing Hatton's Psalter to Taylor on stylistic grounds, the argument being made by the citation of parallels in phrasing and imagery between the Psalter and Taylor's undisputed works.

275 Gathorne-Hardy, Robert. "Jeremy Taylor's Bibliography." TLS, October 2, 1930, p. 782.

In part a response to No. 319. Also sets forth some newer information since the publication of No. 228, and raises questions about Taylor as a possible translator of Pascal and his authorship of A Guide to the Penitent, 1664.

276 Gathorne-Hardy, Robert. "Jeremy Taylor: Undescribed First Editions." TLS, September 15, 1932, p. 648.

Lists several items omitted from No. 228 and some corrections. All this information was later incorporated into No. 270.

277 Gosse, Edmund. Jeremy Taylor. London: Macmillan, 1904.

A full biography and literary study in the "English Men of Letters" series. This is still a useful brief biography, though somewhat inaccurate.

278 Greenslade, B. D. "Jeremy Taylor in 1655." N&Q, 196 (1951): 130.

Quotes a letter from Henry Hammond to Gilbert Sheldon which supports the belief that Taylor was imprisoned in Chepstow Castle in 1655.

279 Harris, L. J. "Lampeter Additions to the Bibliography of Jeremy Taylor." The Library, 5th series, 28 (1973): 243-244.

Notes a unique edition of Episcopacy Asserted and also other copies of Taylor's works in this library which were not included in No. 270.

280 Heber, Mrs. Reginald. The Life of Reginald Heber, 2 vols. London: J. Murray, 1830 (passim).

Many references to Bishop Heber's interest in Taylor and his work on the collected edition (Nos. 174 and 186).

281 Heber, Reginald. The Life of Jeremy Taylor, 2 vols. London: James Duncan & R. Priestley, 1824.

This biography of Taylor prints many of his letters and is essentially the biography which appeared as part of No. 178.

282 Heber, Reginald. The Life of Jeremy Taylor. Hartford, Conn.: F. J. Huntington, 1832.

This is the first American edition taken from the third London edition of No. 281.

283 Henson, H. H. Jeremy Taylor: 1613-1667. London: S.P.C.K. (Typical English Churchmen series), 1902.

A general biographical appreciation of Taylor which provides no new information, although it does place Taylor within the Anglican tradition.

284 Hone, Richard. Lives of James Usher, Henry Hammond, John Evelyn, and Thomas Wilson. London: J. W. Parker, 1842 (pp. 193-194, 203).

Prints a letter from Taylor to Evelyn, 25 February 1658, and a portion of another letter.

285 Johnston, Thomas J., John L. Robinson, Robert Wyse Jackson. A History of the Church of Ireland. London: A.P.C.K., 1953 (pp. 196, 204-208, 226, 272, 276).

Deals primarily with Taylor's disputes with the thirty-six non-conformist ministers in his diocese and gives him high marks for his handling of the situation.

286 Kennett, White. A Register and Chronicle
Ecclesiastical and Civil from the Restoration
of King Charles II. London, 1728 (passim).

Records Taylor's official and public actions and
appointments from the Restoration onwards.

287 Kerr, W. S. "Bishop Jeremy Taylor." Spectator, 122
(1919): 730.

A response to Nos. 406 and 414 and a defense of
Taylor's conduct in dealing with the non-conformist
ministers in Ulster.

288 Keynes, Geoffrey. "Bibliography of Jeremy Taylor."
TLS, October 9, 1930, p. 810.

Answers No. 275 and points out that the evidence to
be found on an advertisement leaf is no real evidence
of Taylor being a translator of Pascal.

289 Lawlor, H. J. "Two Letters of Jeremy Taylor."
Church of Ireland Gazette, 43 (1901):
482-483.

Reprints letters by Taylor: 11 October 1660 to
Capt. Charles Twig and 27 October 1660 to Lord
Montgomery.

290 Leslie, James B., and Henry B. Swanzy.
Biographical Succession Lists of the
Clergy of the Diocese of Down. Ennis Killen: R. H.
Ritchie, 1936 (p. 9).

S.E.; see No. 314.

291 Mant, Richard. History of the Church in Ireland,
2 vols. London: J. W. Parker, 1840 (passim, esp. 1,
Chap. 9).

N.C.

292 The Manuscripts of the Dukes of Rutland,
4 vols., ed. H. C. Maxwell Lyte, et al. London: Eyre &
Spottiswoode, 1888-1905 (2: 5-6).

Volumes one and two appear as Appendices 4 and 5 to
the 12th Report of the Historical Manuscripts
Commission; volume 3 appears as Appendix 1 to the 14th
Report of the Commission; volume 4 appears as an

unnumbered volume. Prints a letter from Taylor to the
Countess of Rutland on 21 June 1658, written from
Annesley where Taylor was in attendance on the
Countess' daughter.

293 Maxwell, Constantia. A History of Trinity
     College , Dublin. Dublin: Trinity College Press, 1946
     (pp. 70-71).

     Brief discussion of Taylor as Chancellor; see also No.
     262.

294 May, E. H. A Dissertation on the Life, Theology,
     and Times of Dr. Jeremy Taylor. London: Bemrose & Sons,
     1892.

     Briefly treats Taylor's biography and devotes most of
     its space to careful summaries of Taylor's works and
     a general discussion of the theology found in them.
     This work clearly places Taylor in the mainstream of
     Anglican thought and notes the instances where he was
     in advance of his age. May's attitude can be seen by
     his concluding statement: "Taylor most nearly of any
     religious writer approached perfection."

295 Newcome, Henry. Autobiography, 2 vols., ed. R.
     Parkinson. London: Chetham Society, 1852 (2: 312).

     Recounts that a Mrs. Turner saw a crucifix above the
     altar in Taylor's study at Uppingham.

296 Nicolson, Marjorie. "New Material on Jeremy
     Taylor." Philological Quarterly, 8 (1929): 321-334.

     A discussion, with quoted extracts, from references
     to Taylor in the Conway letters. This material
     eventually appeared in No. 255.

297 Phillips, Walter Allison, et al. The History of the
     Church of Ireland, 3 vols. Oxford: OUP,1933 (3: 121-147,
     171, 276-277).

     General sketch of Taylor and Bramhall as eminently
     representative of the Church of Ireland and gives some
     details of Taylor's efforts at rebuilding churches.

298 Pocock, Edward. Theological Works, 2 vols., ed.
L. Twells. London: Twells and Gosling, 1740 (vol. 1, passim).

Taylor is mentioned in Twells' introductory account
of Pocock's life.

299 Porter, Classon. Ulster Biographical Sketches,
2nd series. Belfast, 1884.

A brief life of Taylor, especially his life in
Ireland.

300 Printing and the Mind of Man, ed. John Carter and
Percy H. Muir. London: Cassell, 1967 (p. 81).

A brief discussion of the 1650 edition of HL both as a
work of devotion and as an example of
seventeenth-century printing.

301 The Rawdon Papers, ed. E. Berwick. London: J. Nichols
& Son, 1819 (passim).

A collection of letters to and from Archbishop
Bramhall, Sir Arthur Rawdon his son-in-law, and Sir
Arthur Rawdon his grandson. They concern Irish
affairs, mainly, and Taylor is often referred to after
the Restoration.

302 Reeves, William. Ecclesiastical Antiquities of Down,
Connor, and Dromore. Dublin: Hodges & Smith, 1847
(pp. 72, 103, 372).

Deals with Taylor's episcopal duties in Ireland and
particularly matters of property and income.

303 Scott, Charles. "Bishop Jeremy Taylor at His
Visitation." Irish Church News, 2 (1894): 213-216.

A detailed account of several parishes in the Belfast
area during the Interregnum and Restoration indicating
how lawlessly Anglican ministers were expelled and how
Taylor was much less intolerant in restoring order to
the church than he is alleged to have been.

304 Seaver, J. Montgomery. Taylor Genealogy.
Philadelphia: American Historical-Geneol. Soc., 1929
(p. 18 and passim).

A genealogical survey of the American branches of the
Taylor family which draws slight connections with the
family of Jeremy Taylor.

305 Seymour, St. John D. The Puritans in Ireland, 1647-
1661. Oxford: The Clarendon Press, 1912 (pp. 169-177,
196-198, 201-203).

Discusses Taylor's coming to Ireland under the patronage
of Lord Conway in 1659 and devotes special attention to
adversely criticizing Gosse's biography (No. 277).
There is also discussion of Taylor's troubles with the
Ulster Presbyterians when he became Bishop of Down.

306 Simpson, W. J. Sparrow. Archbishop Bramhall.
London: The Macmillan Co., 1927 (passim).

Provides a good deal of information about Taylor in
connection with church government, Irish politics, and
his dealings with Archbishop Bramhall.

307 Smith, Logan Pearsall. "Jeremy Taylor." Life and
Letters, 2 (1929): 245-262.

A brief, but well done, appreciation of Taylor.

308 Smith, Logan Pearsall. "Jeremy Taylor." The Dial,
86 (1929): 271-283.

Same as No. 307.

309 Stevenson, John. Two Centuries of Life in Down:
1600-1800. Belfast: McCaw, Stevenson & Orr Ltd.,1920
(p. 140).

A very brief account of Taylor's ejection of
Presbyterian ministers when he became Bishop of
Down and Connor.

310 "Stewart's 'Introduction to the Encyclopaedia.'"
Edinburgh Review, 27 (1816): 242-244.

Discusses Taylor's toleration, scholasticism, and
casuistry, but views his rhetorical excesses with
disfavor.

311 Stokes, J., and A. E. Stokes. Just Rutland.
Uppingham: John Hawthorn, 1953 (pp. 18-19).

Brief account of Taylor as a parish priest in
Uppingham and also suggests he fled from arrest in
Uppingham to Hatton's home, Kirby Hall, Northampton.

312 Stranks, C. J. "Jeremy Taylor." Church Quarterly
Review, 131 (1940): 31-63.

Biographical; an early version of No. 313.

313 Stranks, C. J. The Life and Writings of Jeremy
Taylor. London: S.P.C.K., 1952.

The most recent and thorough study of Taylor's life
and works. Stranks prints a large amount of Taylor's
correspondence, and although the work has been often
criticized, it is still the standard modern biography.

314 Swanzy, Henry B. Biographical Succession Lists of
the Diocese of Dromore. Belfast: R. Carswell & Son Ltd.,
1923 (pp. 4-5).

S.E., see No. 290.

315 Vinycomb, John. "Arms of the Bishoprics of
Ireland." Ulster Journal of Archaeology, 3 (1856):
104-106.

S.E.

316 Ware, Sir James. Complete Works, 2 vols., ed.
Walter Harris. Dublin, 1764 (1: 125, 128,
209-213).

Mentions Taylor's funeral sermon for Bramhall, his
Chancellorship of Trinity College, and gives a brief
biography.

317 Welcher, Jeanne K. "John Evelyn to Jeremy Taylor,
April 1656." N&Q, 214 (1969): 375.

Demonstrates the source as Gassendi for Evelyn's state-
ment to Taylor about the former's proposed translation
of Lucretius.

318 Wheeldon, J. The Life of Bishop Taylor, and the
Pure Spirit of His Writings. . . . London: G. Bigg, 1793.

A biography and study, relying heavily on quotations,
which portrays Taylor as a pious and astute churchman
and bishop, and stresses the devotional aspect of all
his writings.

319 White, Newport B. "Jeremy Taylor's Bibliography."
TLS, September 25, 1930, p. 758.

Offers four corrections to Gathorne-Hardy's
bibliography published in No. 228 based on the
holdings of Marsh's Library, Dublin.

320 Whitelocke, Bulstrode. Memorials of the English
Affairs. London, 1732 (p. 130).

Reports that "Dr. Taylor" was among those taken
prisoner after the siege of Cardigan Castle in 1644.

321 Williams, William P. "The First Edition of Holy
Living: An Episode in the Seventeenth-Century English
Book Trade." The Library, 5th series, 28 (1973): 99-107.

An account of the political and booktrade machinations
surrounding the first publication of HL in 1650, and
showing that all variant 1650 copies are of the same
edition and that no priority of variants can be
established.

322 Williamson, Hugh Ross. Jeremy Taylor. London: Dobson,
1952.

A study of the life and writings of Taylor; bright and
perceptive study, though perhaps lacking in depth and
scholarship.

323 Willmott, Robert E. Aris. Bishop Jeremy Taylor,
His Predecessors, Contemporaries, and
Successors. London: Parker & Son, 1847; 1848.

A full-scale study of Taylor and his milieu. Although
it is by now dated, it is still a valuable book for the
placing of Taylor in his times.

324 Worley, F. Jeremy Taylor: A Sketch of His Life ·
and Times. London: Longmans, 1904.

A "popular" study of Taylor's works and an attempt to
indicate his theology so that it can be grasped by the
educated layman. Sets Taylor in the context of his
times and avoids detailed biography. Worley deplores
the obscurity into which he believes Taylor has
fallen.

325 Worthington, John. Diary and Correspondence, 3
vols., ed. J. Crossley. London: Chetham Soc., 1847-1886
(1: 135, 171, 301).

Deals primarily with Taylor's appointment of George
Rust as Dean of Down in 1661. All references are
tangential since the main concern of Worthington was
Rust and his circle, not Taylor.

II. B. THEOLOGICAL STUDIES

326 (Anon.). Bishop Taylor's Warning Voice. London:
Rivington, 1843.

N.C.

327 (Anon.). A Brief Vindication [Of Taylor]. London,
1850.

N.C.

328 (Anon.). Catholic Faith and Practice: Wherein the
Character of the Excellent Bishop Taylor
is Fully Vindicated from the Unfair Representation
of Mr. Phillips in his Life of Cardinal Pole
London, 1765.

Demonstrates how Phillips misrepresented Taylor when he
tried to use Taylor as an authority for the toleration
of Roman Catholics.

329 (Anon.). "The Love of Jeremy Taylor." The Academy,
57 (1899): 185-186.

Discusses Charles Lamb's praise of Taylor to his friend
Robert Lloyd with extract of their correspondence and
quotations from Taylor.

330 (Anon.). Incipit: "Notwithstanding the great
variety. . . ." Bodleian Library. G. A. Oxon. b. 17.
item 14. Oxford, 1772.

A printed broadside concerned with the subscription of
the 39 Articles controversy, noting the pertinence of
Taylor's exposition of the Ninth Article in UN and
printing an extract from that work.

331 (Anon.). A Reply to a Pamphlet, entitled,
the Protestant Flail; or a Defence
(Grounded upon Scripture) of a Letter to the
Clergy of Northumberland; in further
Vindication of Bp. Taylor. Newcastle-upon-Tyne,
1735.

N.C.

332 Addison, James T. "Jeremy Taylor, Preacher and
Pastor." Historical Magazine of the Protestant
Episcopal Church, 21 (1952) : 148-190.

A superficial summary of Taylor's life and works,
ostensibly to enhance Taylor's reputation with modern
Christians.

333 Addleshaw, G. W. O. The High Church Tradition: A
Study of Liturgical Thought of the
Seventeenth Century. London: Faber,1941 (passim).

Points out that the High Church divines were mainly
concerned to re-establish learned theology in the
Church of England because of its loss during the
Reformation controversies. This work is a general
study of liturgical attitudes and Taylor is regularly
cited, especially An Apology for Liturgy (1649).

334 Allison, C. F. "Pastoral Cruelty of Jeremy Taylor's
Theology." The Modern Churchman, n.s. 15 (January,
1972): 123-131.

Attempts to show Taylor's views on sin and redemption
to be non-Anglican and heretical, but this is largely
done by polemic and by passages from Taylor's works
which are wrenched from all context.

335 Allison, C. F. The Rise of Moralism. London:
S.P.C.K., 1967 (passim).

Divides Anglican doctrine in the seventeenth century
between early orthodoxy and later Socinianism; Taylor
is seen as a leading member of the latter group and
fatally flawed (pelagian) in his doctrine because of
his unorthodox views on justification.

336 Barr, Lois E. "The Non-Biblical Learning of Jeremy
Taylor, with Special Reference to the Sermons,
Holy Living, and Holy Dying." Doctoral
dissertation, University of North Carolina, 1954.
[McNamee, p. 288].

S.E.

337 Bentley, G. B. "Jeremy Taylor's Ductor
Dubitantium." Theology, 50 (1947): 183-186.

Repeats the biography of Taylor, as known from Heber,
for the 1650's and 1660's and shows how Taylor's
view of casuistry differed from traditional
Roman Catholic ones and how Taylor's contribution
to the subject is the application of reason to
individual cases.

338 Blewett, William Edison. "Jeremy Taylor:
Baconian, Socinian, and Arminian Influences upon
His Thought." DA, 25 (1964): 1373. [Mich. State Univ.].

Taylor's casuistry seems to be to supply a lack
noted by Bacon, and Taylor's patrons had connections
with known Baconians; Taylor rejected Socinianism but
has many Arminian characteristics.

339 Bolton, F. R. The Caroline Tradition of the
Church in Ireland. London: S.P.C.K., 1958 (passim).

Discusses the Caroline backgrounds of Anglicanism with
special reference to the Restoration in Ireland and
Taylor's place in it. Bolton believes Taylor was the
author of the Irish "Form of Consecration of Churches,"
issued in 1666 and also provides much new biographical
evidence of Taylor in Ireland.

340 Bradford, A. H. "Holy Living and Holy Dying."
Outlook, 57 (1897): 420-422.

General and popular summary and appreciation of these
two works which ranks them second below the Imitation
of Christ as major devotional works.

341 Brush, J. W. "The Liberty of Prophesying: A
Tercentenary Essay of Appreciation." Crozier
Quarterly, 25 (1948): 216-223.

Places this work in contemporary context and
states Taylor's plea for toleration is part of the
broad road of Anglican thought of Chillingworth and

Hooker; also points to the breadth of knowledge of
Christian history shown by Taylor and shows how his
views provoked attacks on the work from all shades
of opinion including Anglicans, and points to the
pertinence of the work for the twentieth century.

342   Burns, Norman T. Christian Mortalism from Tyndale
      to Milton. Cambridge, Mass.: Harvard Univ. Press, 1972
      (pp. 91, 97, 103).

      Briefly treats Taylor's recommending the Apostles'
      Creed as the best main basis for faith, and his belief
      in some measure of reward for the soul after death and
      before resurrection.

343   Carpenter, W. Boyd. The Prophets of Christendom.
      London: Hodder, 1884 (pp. 225-239).

      Rather sketchy biography of Taylor relying entirely on
      secondary sources and repeating the "old chestnuts,"
      myths, and legends concerning Taylor.

344   Clarke, W. K. L., ed. Liturgy and Worship.
      London: S.P.C.K., 1932 (pp. 190, 248, 254, 573, 625).

      Mentions Taylor's composition of alternative
      prayer books during the Interregnum, quotes some of his
      views on fasting, and reprints a prayer for the
      visitation of the sick which has been incorporated
      into the Canadian Office and American Prayerbook.

345   Clert-Rolland, L. "Jeremy Taylor et la tolérance
      religieuse au XVIIe siecle." Revue d'historie et de
      philosophie religieuses, 49 (1969): 257-264.

      Study of LP which views it from a perspective
      not only of its English forerunners and analogues,
      primarily Milton and Chillingworth, but also
      in the context of continental religious tolerance.

346   Coleridge, Samuel Taylor. "Thoughts on the Church."
      The Christian Observer, 45 (1845): 328-329.

      Thinks Taylor sound on matters of discipline
      and the Eucharist, and a great stylist, but he
      would not trust him on matters of Original Sin where he
      believes him to be greatly in error.

347 Cox, Gerald H., III. "A Re-evaluation of Jeremy
Taylor's Holy Living and Holy Dying." Neuphilologische
Mitteilungen, 73 (1972): 836-848.

Believes HD has overshadowed HL among critics for
emotional reasons and tries to correct this by
focusing on Taylor's teachings about deathbed
repentance and the importance of living well for
dying well.

348 Cross, F. L. The Oxford Movement and
the Seventeenth Century. London: S.P.C.K., 1933
(passim).

Taylor's influence on the Oxford Movement is assessed,
along with that of other divines of the period; he
is particularly noted for DD, LP, and his writings
about the Eucharist and the Papacy.

349 Cuming, G. J. The Durham Book: Being the First
Draft of the Revision of the Book of Common Prayer
in 1661. London: Oxford Univ. Press, 1961 (passim).

The phrasing of Collection of Offices (1658) is
frequently compared or contrasted with that of the
1661 revision of the Book of Common Prayer.

350 Cuming, G. J. A History of Anglican Liturgy.
London: Macmillan, 1969 (pp. 136, 147-148, 150, 152,
170, 173, 182, 186, 189).

Discusses briefly Taylor's Collection of Offices and
"Form for the Consecration of Churches" in the
historical development of Anglican liturgy; sees
Taylor as a model followed by many.

351 Dargan, Edwin Charles. A History of Preaching,
2 vols. London: Hodder & Son, 1912 (2: 155-159, 163,
167, 169, 179).

Gives a cursory summary of the main facts of Taylor's
life, judges Taylor to be a great writer of ornate
prose, and notes that this style fell from favor.

352 Davison, John. "Tracts on Baptismal Regeneration."
Quarterly Review, 15 (1816): 475-511.

Taylor is cited as an authority on the questions of
baptism as a sacrament and infant baptism.

353 Dowden, E. Puritan and Anglican. London: K. Paul,
Trench, Trubner & Co., 1901 (pp. 197-231).

After some general, but very sensible, comments about
Taylor's style, Dowden discusses LP as an Anglican
eirenicon and contrasts this with Baxter's views
as found in Reliquiae Baxterianae.

354 Dugmore, C. W. Eucharistic Doctrine in England
from Hooker to Waterland. London: S.P.C.K., 1942 (passim).

Cites LP as one of the documents of the increasing
rationalism and toleration in Anglicanism. Another
lengthy discussion seeks to demonstrate that Taylor
changed his Eucharistic views in the course of his
career from high church Laudianism to those called here
"central churchmanship"; also treats the relationship
among Taylor, John Cosin, William Nicholson, and the household of the Earl of Carbery.

355 DuPriest, Travis T., Jr. "The Liturgies of Jeremy
Taylor and Richard Baxter: A Study of Structure,
Language, and Rhythm." DA, 33 (1972): 2323A-2324A.
[Kentucky].

Notes that both authors have been neglected by literary
critics as liturgical writers; and shows how
Taylor's liturgical style manifests his belief that God
deserves the most perfect offering man can make, while
Baxter believed that the Holy Spirit controls such
matters. Taylor is also shown as the most stylistically
ordered of the two authors.

356 Elmen, Paul. "Jeremy Taylor and the Fall of Man."
Modern Language Quarterly, 14 (1953): 139-148.

Discusses Taylor's concept of the Fall in UN and DD
and the controversies his views caused; indicates how
Taylor oversimplified moral problems in an effort to
emphasize man's free choice.

357 Fenn, P. T., Jr. "Latitudinarians and Toleration."
Washington University [St. Louis] Studies (Humanities
Series), 13 (1925): 181-245.

Discusses the toleration of Hales, Chillingworth, and
Taylor, primarily, showing their affinities and their
adherence to the Scriptures and common principles of
right and wrong which they believed united all
Protestants. Also indicates Taylor's belief in
a unity on fundamentals and toleration of diversity
of belief on less central matters.

358 Fisch, Harold. Jerusalem and Albion: The Hebraic
     Factor in Seventeenth Century Literature. London:
     Routledge & K. Paul, 1964 (pp. 173-186, and passim).

     This work uses the concepts of an "Hebraic" style and
     thought in the seventeenth century and particularly
     views Taylor as a "right-wing Anglican" who saw the
     Covenant not in narrow Puritan terms but as offering
     universal salvation. The Hebraic aspects of Taylor's
     style are noted.

359 Foster, J. "The State of Man." Eclectic Review, 25
     (1849): 161-172.

     Taylor's authorship of Contemplations of the State
     of Man is not questioned and thus Foster's castigating
     remarks on the style have little relevance to Taylor and
     are badly dated by later scholarship.

360 Freund, Michael. Die Idee der Toleranz im England
     der grossen Revolution. Halle: M. Niemeyer, 1927 (pp. 43-
     58).

     Discusses Taylor's views on toleration, scepticism and
     rationalism in the context of the Civil War, and
     particularly in relation to John Hales and William
     Chillingworth.

361 Fujimura, Thomas. "Dryden's Religio Laici: An
     Anglican Poem." PMLA, 76 (1961): 205-217.

     Uses DD as evidence of the more limited sphere of
     activity for human reason in Anglicanism and thus
     to show how Dryden can be both fideist and Anglican.

362 George, E. A. Seventeenth Century Men of
     Latitude. New York: Scribner, 1908 (pp. 131-147 and
     passim).

     After a brief summary of Taylor's life, which focuses
     particularly on the Golden Grove years, George engages
     in an analysis of LP largely by copious quotation,
     showing how Taylor was more liberal and more just than
     others, especially in the treatment of heretics,
     creeds, and the Scripture.

363 Greiffenhagen, M. Skepsis und Naturrecht in der
     Theologie Jeremy Taylors, 1613-1667. Hamburg-
     Bergstedt: Reich, Evangelischer Verlag, 1967.

     Offers a general background of scepticism, right

45

reason, and free will with specific examples from and
discussions of Taylor's works. Also discussed is
Taylor's view of nature, his apologetics, and his
pragmatism and humanism. Tries to rescue Taylor from
the generally held low opinion of him as an original
thinker.

364 Grisbrooke, W. Jardine. Anglican Liturgies of the
Seventeenth and Eighteenth Centuries. London: S.P.C.K.,
1958 (pp. 19-36, 183-99, and passim).

Examines Taylor's eucharistic doctrine and liturgical
writing and points out that he is the first to go
"behind" Cranmer and the narrow liturgical tradition of
the western church to make use of the primitive liturgies
and works of the ancient fathers. Disagrees with
Dugmore (No. 354) that Taylor was "central" and
sees his doctrine and practice as exclusive. Reprints
the text of the communion service from A Collection of
Offices.

365 Hammond, T. C. "Post-Reformation Theology in the
Church of Ireland." The Church of Ireland: A. D. 432-
1932. ed. W. Bell and N. D. Emerson. Dublin: P. & P.
Co., 1932 (pp. 100-101).

Taylor is treated in summary manner and he is judged
to be of quick wit, though not always judicial; DD is
thought to have serious flaws.

366 Henson, H. H. Studies in English Religion in the
Seventeenth Century. London: Murray, 1903 (passim).

Treats Taylor's Erastian views on the excommunication of
princes, his break with Romanzcasuistical practice in
DD, and his defense of the Anglican position and
tolerance. Very general remarks on all these subjects.

367 Henson, H. H. The Liberty of Prophesying. New
Haven: Macmillan, 1910 (passim).

The Lyman Beecher Lectures for 1909 and three sermons
by Henson in which he covers much the same ground
Taylor had, but in the context of the post-Tractarian
era.

368 Herndon, Sarah. "The Use of the Bible in Jeremy
Taylor's Works." Doctoral dissertation, New York
University, 1945. [McNamee, p. 287].

S.E.

369 Hoopes, Robert. "Voluntarism in Jeremy Taylor and
the Platonic Tradition." HLQ, 13 (1950): 341-354.

By means of selective quotation Hoopes shows Taylor to
have been at once "victimized" by Thomistic
intellectualism and Scotist voluntarism, and this dual
influence accounts for many of the charges levelled
against him as a confused thinker.

370 Hopkirk, D. S. "A Seventeenth Century Classic:
Jeremy Taylor's Liberty of Prophesying." Reformed
Theological Review, 14 (1955): 81-89.

A careful study of this work as one of the significant
accommodationist texts of the century.

371 Hughes, H. Trevor. "Jeremy Taylor and John Wesley."
London Quarterly and Holborn Review, 174 (1949):
296-304.

Discusses the importance of HL and HD in Wesley's
spiritual development and attempts to delineate the
nature of Wesley's "use" of these works.

372 Hughes, H. Trevor. The Piety of Jeremy Taylor.
London: Macmillan, 1960.

Deals with Taylor's theology of ministry, toleration,
original sin, and the sacraments and then presents his
piety in both his general principles (law, conscience,
and sin and penance) and pragmatic circumstances (i.e.,
the Christian in society). A good general theological
discussion, though tending toward the hagiographic.

373 Humphrey, W. G. Jeremy Taylor's Holy Living and
Holy Dying. London: Murray (St. James Lectures, 1st
series), 1875; 1877.

Popular appreciation of these two works as devotional
masterpieces.

374 Inge, William Ralph. The Platonic Tradition in
English Religious Thought. London: Longmans, Green, 1926
(pp. 39, 47).

States that Taylor belonged to a liberal comprehensive,
but not Platonic, movement in English religious thought
which followed the Reformation.

375 'Irish Presbyterian, An.' "Church and State."
Spectator, 122 (1919): 593-594.

Yet one more anti-Taylor assertion prompted by No. 406;
see also Nos. 287 and 414.

376 Jordan, W. K. The Development of Religious
Toleration in England, 4 vols. London and Cambridge,
Massachusetts: Harvard Univ. Press, 1932-1940 (vol. 4,
passim).

In this exhaustive survey of the subject Taylor is cited
as having made a large contribution to the development
of a theory of toleration and to have influenced future
Anglican thought on the subject, and he concludes that
even Taylor's subsequent difficulties in Ireland do
not diminish the importance of his work.

377 Kerr, N. S. Who Persecuted? Episcopalian and
Presbyterian in Ulster. Belfast: W. Erskine Mayne, 1947
(passim).

A study and defense of Taylor's activities as a bishop
against the Presbyterian clergy who opposed him; deals
with the question of tolerance in a practical
situation.

378 Lewis, C. S. The Great Divorce. London: G. Bles, 1945
(pp. 60-61).

Brief mention of Taylor's use of the word "refrigerium,"
also used by Prudentius.

379 Ludolf, Heinrich Wilhelm. Christ or Anti-Christ.
London, 1758.

N.C.

380 McAdoo, H. R. The Spirit of Anglicanism. New
York: Scribner, 1965 (pp. 49-80 and passim).

Treats Taylor in the same chapter on moral theology as
Andrewes and Sanderson and sees Taylor as closest to
Chillingworth and the Cambridge Platonists; also his
theology is practical and relevant in intent and this is
partly because of his interest in liturgies and
devotions; he is concerned with personal relationships
and the continuity of Anglicanism.

381 McAdoo, H. R. The Structure of Caroline Moral
Theology. London: Longmans, 1949 (passim).

Study of the Caroline divines' attempts to provide
a moral theology which was both catholic and reformed,
rational and pious, frequently citing Taylor for
mediating statements and for his casuistical works.

382 McGee, J. Sears. The Godly Man in Stuart England.
New Haven: Yale Univ. Press, 1976 (passim).

In this study of Anglican and Puritan views from 1620 to
1670, Taylor is cited as the moderate pious churchman.

383 Mackenzie, E. H. "Golden Grove." TLS, November 20,
1937, p. 891.

Points out that Taylor's Golden Grove was probably named
after not only Lord Carbery's house in Wales but also
the influential moral treatise published by his uncle,
William Vaughan, in 1600.

384 McLachlan, H. John. Socinianism in Seventeenth
Century England. London: Oxford Univ. Press, 1951
(pp. 87-89, 98).

Briefly attempts to show that LP is the direct
offspring of Chillingworth's Religion of Protestants,
and that Taylor, Chillingworth, and Hales were
forerunners of the Cambridge Platonists.

385 Merriman, Daniel. "Jeremy Taylor and Religious
Liberty in the Church of England." Proceedings of
the Worcester, Mass. Antiquarian Society,
17 (1907): 93-124.

Places Taylor in the number of those who worked for
religious toleration from within the established
church, and after a rather extensive biographical
sketch, LP is summarized in detail and it is seen to
be a contribution to religious freedom equal to, but
quite unlike, those of Milton and Roger Williams.

386 Meyrick, Frederick. Moral Theology of the Church of
Rome. Baltimore: J. Robinson,1856 (pp. ix-xii, 23, 91,
235-237, 250-252, 261-264).

Deals with Taylor's connections with, and opposition to,
Roman moral theology, particularly casuistry as found
in DD.

49

387 More, Paul Elmer, and Frank L. Cross. Anglicanism:
the Thought and Practice of the Church of
England, Illustrated from the Literature of
the Seventeenth Century. London: S.P.C.K., 1935 (passim).

This anthology of seventeenth-century English churchmen
quotes Taylor often on a variety of subjects and
provides brief comments.

388 Nossen, Robert. "Jeremy Taylor: Seventeenth-
Century Theologian". Anglican Theological
Review, 42 (1960): 28-39.

Concerned only with Taylor's theological opinions regarding
death, this article treats HD exclusively showing how Taylor
went beyond the old Ars tradition, and that although he was
severe on theoretical matters he was tender and helpful when
dealing with specific cases.

389 O'Connor, Sister Mary Catherine. The Art of
Dying Well: The Development of the Ars
Moriendi. New York: Columbia Univ. Press, 1942 (pp. 38,
208-210).

Points out how even though Taylor tried to break with
the old Ars tradition in HD, he was unable to
completely eradicate it from his work.

390 Packer, John W. The Transformation of Anglicanism,
1643-1660. Manchester: Manchester Univ. Press, 1969
(passim).

This book is particularly devoted to Henry Hammond, but
Taylor is regularly compared with him. Packer is also
interested in Taylor's views on toleration, his desire
for a comprehensive church, and his leadership of the
Laudian party.

391 Peck, George. "Religious Tolerance in Jeremy
Taylor." Doctoral dissertation, Western Reserve
University, 1943. [McNamee, p. 287].

Complete study of Taylor as representative and important
in the development of religious tolerance in his age.

392 Perkins, E. B. "Jeremy Taylor on Gambling." London
Quarterly and Holborn Review, 184 (1959): 140-144.

A brief survey of gaming in the seventeenth century
and of Taylor's stand on this subject in Book
Four of DD.

393 Peterson, Raymond Alfred, Jr. "Jeremy Taylor on
Conscience and Law." Anglican Theological Review,
48 (1966): 243-263.

A careful book-by-book discussion of DD indicating
Taylor's status as a moral theologian and calling
for an end to the neglect of this work; indicates
the main threads of his moral theology, particularly
his probabiliarism and nominalism.

394 Peterson, Raymond Alfred, Jr. "Jeremy Taylor's
Theology of Worship." Anglican Theological Review,
46 (1964): 204-216.

Examines Taylor's liturgical, homiletical, and
ascetical writings; sees Apology for Liturgy as his
attack on the Directory of Public Worship
and that Taylor believed the proper public
worship of God required set forms; views
Taylor's preaching, particularly Eniautos,
to be concerned with Christian sanctification;
stresses Taylor's interest in "mental prayer" in
GE, HD, and HL, and sees a connection with St. Francis
de Sales.

395 Peterson, Raymond Alfred, Jr. "The Theology of
Jeremy Taylor: An Investigation of the Temper of
Caroline Anglicanism." DA, 21 (1961): 3178. [Union
Theological Sem.].

States that Taylor is important not because he was a
theologian of the first rank but because most of the
elements of seventeenth-century Anglican thought are
present in his writings, making him the representative
Caroline divine.

396 Phillips, Thomas. The History of the Life of
Reginald Pole, 2 vols. Oxford: W. Jackson, 1764 (2:
85-86).

LP is quoted as an authority for the total toleration
of Roman Catholics; see also Nos. 328 and 398.

397 Powicke, F. J. "Jeremy Taylor: His Doctrine of
Toleration." Constructive Quarterly, 3 (1915):
657-677.

Taylor was tolerant theologically but intolerant
ecclesiastically; he spoke for the tolerance of
differing opinions but demanded uniformity in the
outward aspects of religion.

398 Ridley, Glocester. *A Review of Mr. Phillips' History of the Life of Reginald Pole*. London: J. Whiston and E. White, 1766 (pp. 258-264).

Quotes a long passage from Section XX of LP to show how Phillips has misrepresented Taylor's attitude toward the toleration of Roman Catholics; see No. 396.

399 Sanderson, Robert. *Works*, 6 vols., ed. W. Jacobson. Oxford: Oxford Univ. Press, 1854 (2: 155; 4: 2, 7, 9, 12, 22; 5: 80; 6: 381-2, 386-89, 459-60).

Notes the parallels and affinities between Taylor's works on devotion and conscience and Sanderson's; makes references to Taylor's view of Original Sin in Sanderson's letters (to Barlow, 28 September 1656 and 17 September 1657), and reprints the "Answer to a Question" signed in 1647 by Sanderson, Taylor, and other Anglican clergy.

400 Sharp, T. *A Reply to a Pamphlet*. Newcastle-upon-Tyne, 1735.

N.C.

401 Slights, Camille. "Ingenious Piety; Anglican Casuistry of the Seventeenth Century." *Harvard Theological Review*, 63 (1970): 409-432.

General survey of seventeenth-century English casuistry, with particular reference to Taylor and Sanderson.

402 Slights, Camille. "To Stand Inquiring Right": The Casuistry of Donne's *Satyre III*. *Studies in English Literature*, 12 (1972), 85-101.

A discussion of the Donne poem, treating Taylor as a typical Anglican casuist and noting how Donne dealt with the differences between Roman and Anglican casuistry.

403 Steffan, T. G. "The Ethical Reason of Jeremy Taylor." *Summaries of Doctoral Dissertations, University of Wisconsin*, 3 (1938): 306-308. [McNamee, p. 287].

Taylor accepts the "reason-faith alliance" of Hooker, and his practicality causes him to dislike abstract speculation; his debt to St. Francis of Sales is noted; Taylor is important because of his synthesis of various strands of thought.

404 Steffan, T. G. "Jeremy Taylor's Criticism of
Abstract Speculation." University of Texas Studies
in English, 1940, pp. 96-108.

See No. 403.

405 Stephen, Sir James. Horae Sabaticae, 1st series.
London: Macmillan & Co., 1892 (pp. 226-285).

Charges Taylor with unintellectuality and finds his
use of language too vague and confusing; manifests the
typical late nineteenth-century dislike of his thought
and style.

406 Strachey, J. St. Loe. "Church and State."
Spectator, 122 (1919): 487-488.

Discussion of the concept of a national church citing LP
as expressing the "very spirit" of "undenominationalism";
"undenominationalism"; responded to by Nos. 287 and 414.

407 Stranks, C. J. Anglican Devotion. London: SCM Press,
1961 (pp. 64-95 and passim).

Notes that HL was produced to supply the devotional
needs of Anglicans since the fall of the Church of
England from power, and HD specifically for Lady
Carbery; points to the simplicity of the structure of
both and their practicality; stresses Taylor's belief
in man's reasonableness.

408 Stranks, C. J. "Sermons by Jeremy Taylor." TLS,
September 27, 1934, p. 655.

Mentions Coleridge's reference to an unpublished folio
manuscript of sermons by Taylor; notes that almost no
scholars have mentioned this since and asks help in
locating it.

409 Sykes, Norman. Old Priest and New Presbyter.
Cambridge: Cambridge Univ. Press, 1956 (pp. 58, 68,
78, 106, 124).

Episcopacy Asserted is regularly cited, and by
implication Taylor becomes one of the official spokes-
men for the episcopal party in seventeenth-century
England.

410   Symonds, H. E.   The Council of Trent and Anglican
      Formularies.   London: Oxford Univ. Press, 1933.

      N.C.

411   Todd, J. H.   "Original Letter of Bishop Jeremy
      Taylor on Theological Studies."   The Irish
      Ecclesiastical Journal, no. 102 (January, 1849):
      198-199.

      Prints a letter from Taylor to Mr. Graham, 13 June 1659;
      with notes and commentary.

412   Tulloch, J.   "Jeremy Taylor and The Liberty of
      Prophesying."   Contemporary Review, 9 (1868):
      245-260, 519-539.

      Discusses the work in the context of the growth of
      rationalism in England and of Taylor's life; relies
      heavily on Heber's biography (No. 281); preliminary
      form of the material in No. 413.

413   Tulloch, J.   Rational Theology and Christian
      Philosophy, 2 vols.   London: W. Blackwood & Sons, 1874
      (passim, esp. 1: 344-410).

      Points out that Taylor only belongs to the history of
      Latitudinarianism because of LP and that the remainder
      of his writings are not of the same nature; summarizes
      his life to show how his conduct was often at variance
      with Latitudinarian views.   An important, full, and
      thoughtful treatment of Taylor.

414   "Ulster."   Church and State.   Spectator, 122
      (1919):   593.

      Accuses Taylor of injustice and a lack of toleration in
      his dealings with the Ulster non-conformists; answered
      by No. 287.

415   Wesley, John.   Journal, 8 vols., ed. Nehemiah
      Curnack.   London: C. H. Kelly, 1909-1916 (1: 15-16, 32,
      42, 47, 51, 83, 96, 281-82, 419; 5: 117; 8: 270-271).

      Shows the importance of HL and HD in Wesley's
      spiritual development and the framing of his "Oxford
      Rules."

416 Wesley, John. Letters, 8 vols., ed. John Telford.
London: The Epworth Press, 1931 (1: 19, 20, 21, 46;
4: 123, 298).

As in No. 415.

417 Whewell, William. Lectures on the History of
Moral Philosophy. London: Parker & Son, 1862 (pp. 18-30).

N.C.

418 Wiley, Margaret. "Jeremy Taylor, the Sceptic as
Churchman." Western Humanities Review, 4 (1950):
3-17.

Points out that Taylor's scepticism probably produced
the tolerant, reasonable, and non- dogmatical
character of his thought so frequently noted by
scholars; his scepticism led to his concern for the
practical rather than the abstract.

419 Wiley, Margaret. "Jeremy Taylor, the Sceptic as
Churchman." The Subtle Knot. London: Allen & Unwin,
1952.

Reprint of No. 418.

420 Wiley, Margaret. "Scepticism in the Writings of
John Donne, Richard Baxter, Jeremy Taylor, Sir
Thomas Browne, and Joseph Glanvill." Doctoral
dissertation, Radcliffe, 1940. [McNamee, p. 272].

S.E.

421 Williams, Roger. Complete Writings, 6 vols., ed.
members of the Narragansett Club. Providence,
1866-1874 (3: iii-xiv; 6: 241, 249, 252).

Bitter attack by Williams on LP and on Taylor's
character followed by the editor's charging Taylor
with intolerance after the Restoration; Mrs. Sadleir
indicates in a letter to Williams that she reads
Taylor's sermons to which Williams retorts and she
answers back with subtlety.

422 Wood, Thomas. English Casuistical Divinity During
the Seventeenth Century, with Special
Reference to Jeremy Taylor. London: S.P.C.K., 1952
(passim).

Overall study of this subject notes how Anglicans had

to create their own reformed casuistry, their works not
being written only for priests but for the laity as
well; also noted is the difficulty of distinguishing
between venial and mortal sins and the abandonment of
this system.

423 Wood, Thomas. "A Great English Casuist." Church
Quarterly Review , 147 (1949): 29-45.

Deals with Sanderson and treats Taylor only as a
figure for comparison.

424 Wood, Thomas. "The Seventeenth Century English
Casuists on Betting and Gambling." Church
Quarterly Review, 149 (1950): 159-174.

Treating this subject DD, Bk. II, chap. I, rule II is
studied and Taylor is found to object to the exchange
of money and waste of time, not to the games
themselves.

II. C. LITERARY STUDIES AND GENERAL STUDIES

425 Addison, Joseph. The Spectator, 5 vols., ed.
Donald F. Bond. Oxford: The Clarendon Press, 1965
(1: 157, 159; 4: 71).

HL and HD are among "Lady Leonora's" books and in "The
Female Library"; a maxim used by Taylor and others is
quoted.

426 Adolph, Robert. The Rise of Modern Prose Style.
Cambridge, Mass.: M.I.T. Press, 1968 (pp. 19, 21, 74,
199, 335).

Cites Taylor's treatment of death in HD as typical of
the seventeenth century's treatment of Seneca.

427 Alford, Henry. Pulpit Eloquence in the
Seventeenth Century. London (YMCA Lectures at
Exeter Hall, no. 13), 1858.

Repeats the usual judgments of Taylor in the context
of his age.

428 Antoine, Sister M. Salome, OSF. The Rhetoric of
Jeremy Taylor's Prose. Washington, D. C.: Catholic U. of
Amer. Press, 1946.

Extensive analysis of the tropes, figures of diction,
and figures of thought in the sermons, with tabular
results as appendices; concludes Taylor achieved a
middle style with oratory in harmony with thought.

429 Arnold, Matthew. The Literary Influence of
Academies. Complete Prose Works of Matthew
Arnold, 10 vols., ed. R. H. Super. Ann Arbor: Univ. of
Mich. Press, 1960- (3: 245-246).

Taylor's prose in his funeral sermon for Lady Carbery
is too poetic and not intellectual enough for Arnold's
taste.

430 Asals, Frederick. "Jeremy Taylor and Hawthorne's
Early Tales." American Transcendental Quarterly,
14 (1972): 15-23.

Shows the close connections between Hawthorne's study
of Taylor's works and the composition of "The Wedding
Knell," "The Minister's Black Veil," and "The Maypole
of Merry Mount."

431 Barry, Alfred. "Jeremy Taylor, the English
Chrysostom. The Classic Preachers of the English
Church, 2nd series, ed. J. E. Kempe. London: J. Murray,
1877 (pp. 55-91).

Praises Taylor's "golden" style with examples drawn
primarily from the sermons and devotional books.

432 Beaty, Nancy Lee. The Craft of Dying: A Study
in the Literary Tradition of the Ars
Moriendi in England. New Haven: Yale Univ. Press, 1970
(pp. 197-270 and passim).

Views HD as the "artistic climax of the tradition" and
shows how Taylor partakes of the old tradition more
than recent scholars have thought; presents an extended
analysis of the work.

433 Brinkley, R. Florence. "Coleridge's Criticism of
Jeremy Taylor." HLQ, 13 (1950): 313-323.

Summarizes the subject and shows that Coleridge
greatly admired Taylor's style and character but
deplored his doctrine, particularly on Original Sin.

434 Churton, Edward. A Letter to Joshua Watson,
Esqr., D. C. L., Giving an Account of
a Singular Literary Fraud Practised on the
Memory of Bishop Jeremy Taylor. London: F. & J. Rivington,
1848.

Full and polemical demonstration that Contemplations
of the State of Man is not by Taylor but by Hackett.

435 Coleridge, Samuel Taylor. Aids to Reflection.
London: Hurst, 1825 (pp. 250, 265-268, 275, 332-333).

Charges Taylor with being an antagonist of the doctrine
of Original Sin; uses Taylor to support his arguments
concerning baptism.

436 Coleridge, Samuel Taylor. Biographia Literaria, 2
vols. London: Fenner, 1817 (2: 10).

Says Plato, Taylor, and Burnet show how poetry need
not be in meter.

437 Coleridge, Samuel Taylor. The Friend, 3 vols.
London: Fenner, 1818 (2: 267-300; 3: 108, 111).

Cites Taylor as a "sublime" author; feels Taylor's
error may have been in being too rational, and again
objects to his views on Original Sin.

438 Coleridge, Samuel Taylor. Letters, 2 vols., ed.
E. H. Coleridge. London: W. Heinemann, 1895 (1: 180-181;
2: 640-641).

Taylor is called "the English Pagan"; charges him
with trying to be all things to all men in his
teachings on repentance and Original Sin.

439 Coleridge, Samuel Taylor. The Literary Remains, 4
vols., ed. H. Nelson Coleridge. London: W. Pickering,
1836-1839 (vol. 3, passim).

Covers a host of concerns but is primarily focused on
praising Taylor's style and spirit and deploring his
theology.

440 Coleridge, Samuel Taylor. "Table Talk." Complete
Works, 7 vols., ed. W. G. T. Shedd. London: W. Pickering,
1853 (6: 295, 328-330, 501).

Remarks that Taylor should be studied for his noble

principles but warns of his errors; thinks Taylor
spoiled his "great and lovely mind" by following Laud
and having popish feelings about church authority.

441 Cox, Gerald H., III. "Tradition and Devotion: The
Prose Meditations of John Donne, Jeremy Taylor, and
Thomas Traherne." DA, 29 (1969): 3970A. [Stanford].

Argues that seventeenth-century devotional prose comes
from the same meditative tradition as poetry as
demonstrated by Louis Martz; these writers' devotions
are shaped by a belief in set forms of worship; HL and
HD are discussed and HL is judged the superior
meditative work.

442 Day, W. G. "Forbidden Embraces: Jeremy Taylor's
Holy Dying." N&Q, 18 (1972): 292-293.

Finds a parallel between Taylor and Montaigne on the
subject of death during copulation.

443 DeQuincey, Thomas. Collected Works, 14 vols., ed.
David Masson. Edinburgh: R. & C. Black, 1889-1890 (1:
348; 8: 100-102, 189-190; 10: 104-110, 125-126; 13: 427).

Mentions Taylor in relation to Lady Carbery and the
Lady Carbery of DeQuincey's times; Taylor is cited as
a sound opponent of popery; the account of Judas in GE
is quoted; Taylor and Browne are seen as the two
greatest rhetorical authors of the seventeenth
century; Taylor and Milton are praised for having
advocated toleration.

444 Doubleday, N. F. "The Theme of Hawthorne's
'Fancy's Show Box'; Certain Parallels Between It
and a Passage in Jeremy Taylor's Ductor
Dubitantium." American Literature, 10 (1938):
341-343.

Compares Hawthorne's work and DD, Part II, Bk. IV,
chap. I, Rule III.

445 Elmen, Paul. "The Fame of Jeremy Taylor." Anglican
Theological Review, 44 (1962): 389-403.

Traces Taylor's reputation from the eighteenth century
to the 1960's; shows the neglect of Taylor in the
earlier period and the increasing interest in him after
Coleridge.

446 Elson, James H. <u>John Hales of Eton</u>. New York: Kings
Crown Press, 1948 (pp. 43, 135-137, 149, 153, 160).

Maintains that Taylor's association with the
Latitudinarians is due only to LP, but that his
devotional, casuistical, and episcopal works properly
represent his views and that the former work is highly
conditioned by the times and contemporary thinkers; his
popularity now, as opposed to that of Hales, is due to
the Romantics' preference for his ornate style.

447 Gardiner, S. R. <u>History of the Great Civil War</u>.
3 vols. London: Longmans, Green, & Co., 1894 (3: 310-312).

Deals primarily with LP and states that "three-
fourths of its argument" was written under the
influence of Chillingworth's <u>Religion of Protestants</u>.

448 Gathorne-Hardy, Robert. "Jeremy Taylor's
Annotations." <u>TLS</u>, September 20, 1947, p. 484.

Describes and reprints annotations in the Gathorne-
Hardy (1650) and King's College, Cambridge (1656)
copies of HL.

449 Gathorne-Hardy, Robert. "Montaigne Among the
English." <u>TLS</u>, September 13, 1947, p. 465.

Notes Taylor's apparent interest in and borrowings from
Montaigne's essays, particularly the Florio translation.

450 Gathorne-Hardy, Robert. <u>Recollections of Logan
Pearsall Smith</u>. London: Constable, 1949 (passim).

Recounts the association of Gathorne-Hardy and Smith
and their mutual interest in Taylor which eventually
led to the publication of No. 228; also much of interest
concerning the antiquarian book trade in copies of
Taylor's works and Smith's personal literary judgments
of Taylor.

451 Glicksman, H. "The Figurative Quality in Jeremy
Taylor's <u>Holy Dying</u>." <u>Sewanee Review</u>, 30 (1922):
488-494.

Brief analysis which tries to show that Taylor's figures
bridge the gulf between the finite and infinite.

452 Gordon, Ian A. The Movement of English Prose.
Bloomington, Indiana: Indiana Univ. Press, 1966 (pp. 8,
49, 116, 117, 160).

Notes Taylor's echoing of the alliterative and paired
word style of Middle English; points out that his style
made great use of the extended simile and this was its
glory and its curse; and notes Arnold's choice of Taylor
for attack because of Taylor's Baroque characteristics.

453 Gray, Thomas. Correspondence, 3 vols., ed. Paget
Toynbee and Leonard Whibley. Oxford: The Clarendon Press,
1935 (2: 719-720, 724).

Gray says Taylor is an apt commentator on marriage and
a more intellectual and feeling writer than the
chop-logics of his own time.

454 Greg, W. W. English Literary Autographs. Oxford:
Oxford Univ. Press, 1932 (item xc).

Facsimile and transcription of a letter from Taylor to
Christopher Hatton about 1643-1645 (BM. Addit. 29581,
fol. 1a) and a headnote.

455 Halewood, William H. The Poetry of Grace. New
Haven: Yale Univ. Press, 1970 (pp. 58, 62, 65, 73).

Attempts to show Puritan views are also to be found in
anti-Puritan authors and cites Taylor on forgiveness of
sin and the theology of devotional literature.

456 Hallam, Henry. Introduction to the Literature of
Europe in the Fifteenth, Sixteenth, and
Seventeenth Centuries. London: J. Murray, 1881-1882 (pp.
447-452).

Provides a detailed summary of LP largely repeating the
judgments and opinions of the learned world to this
time.

457 Hazlitt, William. Lectures Chiefly on the
Dramatic Literature of the Age of
Elizabeth. London: Stoddart & Steuart, 1820. [Lecture no. 7].

Bacon's works are stylistically compared with Browne and
Taylor's and Taylor is noted to be flowing, elaborate,
and enumerative: "he puts his heart into his fancy."

458 Heber, Reginald. Prospectus of a Uniform Edition
of the Whole Works of Jeremy Taylor. London,
1820.

S.E.

459 Huntley, Frank L. "A Background in Folklore for
the 'Blind mouths' Passage in Lycidas." Milton
Newsletter, 1 (1967): 53-55.

Discussion of lines 113-131 of the poem pointing out
that Taylor uses the same fable in Via Intelligentiae.

460 Huntley, Frank L. Jeremy Taylor and the Great
Rebellion: A Study of His Mind and
Temper in Controversy. Ann Arbor: Univ. of Michigan
Press, 1970.

Points out that Taylor did not withdraw from the Civil
War and its controversies but rather that he argued
three distinct cases, at appropriate times: episcopacy
and liturgy (1642 and 1646) while a royal chaplain;
religious freedom (1647) while a private chaplain for
Lord Carbery; and Original Sin (1655-1658) while
imprisoned and attacked by both Anglican and non-
Anglican. Also points to Taylor's moderation,
practicality and charity even in controversy.

461 "J., E." [Untitled article]. Gentleman's
Magazine, 61 (1791): 515-516.

Responds to No. 479 by quoting from No. 318 and
transcribing in full the parish register entry
for Taylor's marriage at Uppingham in 1639.

462 Jackson, Robert Sumner. "The Meditative Life of
Christ: A Study of Background and Structure of
Jeremy Taylor's The Great Exemplar." DA, 19
(1959): 3296. [Univ. of Mich.].

Sees the structure of the work as being similar to
that of the Spiritual Exercises of Ignatius of Loyola.

463 Keble, John. Lectures on Poetry (1832-41), 2
vols., trans. E. K. Francis. Oxford: Clarendon Press,
1912 (1: 50).

Contrasts Burke's description of the Queen of France
with Taylor's of the dying Lady Carbery and ranks Taylor

first for Burke is merely an orator while Taylor's is
"the outpouring of a full heart."

464 King, James Roy. "Certain Aspects of Jeremy
     Taylor's Prose Style." English Studies, 37 (1956):
     197-210.

     A very thorough discussion of style and studies of
     prose style with particular reference to Taylor and
     to the connections between style and thought.

465 King, James Roy. "Jeremy Taylor: Theology and
     Aesthetics." Studies in Six 17th Century Writers.
     Athens, Ohio: Ohio Univ. Press, 1966 (pp. 159-192).

     Studies GE to demonstrate Taylor's liberal and practical
     approach to the question of how Christ could be brought
     effectively into everyman's life; likens the structure
     of the work to Baroque art.

466 King, James Roy. "A Study of Relationships of
     Thematic and Stylistic Variation in Jeremy
     Taylor's Prose." DA, 14 (1954): 525-526. [Penn.].

     Treats Taylor's style in the context of his biography
     and eventually says that Taylor had five different
     styles.

467 Krauth, C. P. "Homiletic Studies, or Pulpit
     Portraits of South, Barrow and Taylor."
     Evangelical Review, 9 (1858): 338-356.

     Very brief biographical sketch followed by a general
     appraisal of his preaching style based only on
     Eniautos; largely a repetition of the traditional
     judgments of Taylor.

468 Kuhre, Walter William. "Natural Law and Prose
     Works of the English Renaissance." DA, 29 (1968):
     1514A. [Penn. State].

     Seeks to find a belief in natural law manifested in the
     prose of various English Renaissance authors; Taylor is
     one of them, though treated as a minor figure.

469 Lamb, Charles. Letters, 3 vols., ed. E. V. Lucas.
     London: J. M. Dent & Sons Ltd., 1935 (1: 74, 256-258,
     285; 2: 23; 3: 366).

     In a letter to Robert Lloyd, Lamb doubts the authenticity

of Contemplations of the State of Man and suggests
passages in Taylor's known works for comparison; also
says selections from Taylor are not possible, all
must be read; and Taylor's views on marriage are also
mentioned.

470 Lowell, James Russell. Works, 16 vols. New York:
A.M.S., 1966 (1: 255; 3: 32-33, 217; 4: 290; 5: 339;
8: 88; 16: 173).

Taylor is compared with Dryden and Shakespeare and it is
said that he would have been John Fletcher's rival had
he lived fifty years earlier; that he is "a kind of
Spenser in a cassock"; and there are various words of
praise for his sermons and the lark simile.

471 "M., C." "The Prose of Jeremy Taylor." American
Monthly Magazine, 7 (1836): 504-508.

Deals only with HL and HD, thinking the latter to be the
best, and saying conventional things about the beauties
of Taylor's prose; comments that Taylor's prose has no
"fiery outbreaks of soul."

472 Manning, Anne. The Masque at Ludlow. London:
Sampson, Low, Son, & Marston, 1866.

Erroneously states that Alice, second Lady Carbery, was
the lady for whom HL and HD were written, rather than
Francis, the first Lady Carbery.

473 Matthiessen, F. O. American Renaissance. New
York: Oxford Univ. Press, 1941 (pp. 16, 104, 120, 127).

Shows how Taylor's style and moderate religious stance
were made use of by American authors, particularly
Emerson.

474 Mazzeo, Joseph Anthony. "Seventeenth-Century English
Prose Style: The Quest for a Natural Style." Mosaic,
6 (1973): 107-144.

Says Taylor mixed high style with excessive figures
to produce a ludicrous effect; considers Taylor so
odd that he is virtually excluded from the mainstream
of seventeenth-century prose.

475 Memorials of Coleorton, 2 vols., ed. William
Knight. Edinburgh: D. Douglas, 1887 (2: 248).

In a letter from an unknown writer Taylor is given
as providing sound authority for infant baptism in
HL.

476 Miner, Earl. The Cavalier Mode from Jonson to
Cotton. Princeton: Princeton Univ. Press, 1971 (p. 133).

States that HL and HD are paranaetical works which
attempt to provide a remedy, or consolation, in troubled
times.

477 Mitchell, William F. English Pulpit Oratory.
London: S.P.C.K., 1932 (passim).

Points out Taylor's use of the classics for illustrative
material and his latinate diction, but notes that unlike
Browne his constructions do not follow classical models;
shows well how Taylor fits between the earlier "witty"
preachers and the later "plain and practical" style.

478 Murray, John. A Publisher and His Friends, 2
vols., ed. Samuel Smiles. London: Murray, 1891 (1:
304-305).

A letter from Coleridge to Murray in which the former
says Taylor and Milton should be considered equal
masters of English prose.

479 "N., R." [Untitled article]. Gentleman's
Magazine, 60 (1790): 301-302; 61 (1791): 313-315.

Attempts to answer No. 260, but does not; says Taylor
was not buried in the choir of Dromore Cathedral as is
popularly believed; also continues the demonstration of
Franklin's plagiarism which was started in No. 488.

480 Nichols, John. Literary Anecdotes. 9 vols.
London: Nichols, 1812-1815 (1: 29, 170, 287, 631-633,
654; 3: 215; 6: 488; 9: 633-634, 765).

Gives some information about the publication of Taylor's
works during the eighteenth century and reprints a
letter commenting on Phillips' Life of Pole (No. 396).

481 Nossen, R. J. "A Critical Study of the Holy Dying
of Jeremy Taylor." Summaries of Doctoral
Dissertations . . . Northwestern University , 19
(1952): 35-39. [McNamee, p. 288].

Sees HD as the culmination of the Ars Moriendi tradition
and as representative of attitudes toward death current
in Taylor's time; it is also a great work of literature
and has influenced later authors; discusses the backgrounds of HD, provides an analysis of its structure, and
traces its reputation.

482 Patrides, C. A. "A Note on Renaissance Plagiarism."
N&Q, 201 (1956): 438-439.

An apparent verbatim theft of a passage from HD by
Richard Stewart is perhaps explained by the latter's
death before his work was published and a citation to
Taylor being omitted.

483 Pollard, Arthur. English Sermons. London: Longmans,
Green and Co. (Writers and Their Works, no. 158), 1963
(pp. 16-19 and passim).

General and popular survey of the topic in which Taylor
is given his usual distinguished place.

484 Quiller-Couch, Arthur. On the Art of Writing.
Cambridge: Cambridge Univ. Press, 1916 (pp. 83-84).

Taylor's style is cited as an example of how even ornate
prose does not have the emotional tension of poetry.

485 Richardson, C. F. English Preachers and English
Preaching. New York: The Macmillan Co., 1928 (passim).

Taylor is cited on various points including listening
to sermons, natural similes, vocabulary, pedantry,
and for the gloominess of some of his descriptions;
his participation in the circle of Katherine Philips
is also noted.

486 Rolland, L. C. "Francois de Sales et Jeremy
Taylor." Revue de Litterature Comparee, 42 (1968):
557-562.

Suggests some of the influences of de Sales on all of
Taylor's writings and indicates that much more work is
needed on this subject.

487 Rollins, G. A. "The Contribution of Jeremy Taylor
to Modern Preaching." Methodist Review, 107
(1924): 274-280.

Attempts to show both how preaching is improved by
the use of imagery and that Taylor is a good example
for study to learn the use of homiletic imagery;
copious quotations from Taylor's works.

488 S., H. [Untitled letter]. Gentleman's Magazine, 51
(1781): 514-515.

Points out that in Franklin's Miscellanies there is a
plagiarism of the story at the very end of the second
printing of LP.

489 Shaw, S. [Untitled article]. Gentleman's Magazine,
2 (1792): 108-109.

Notes that there is no Maidley Hall near Tamworth (see
Nos. 260 and 479) and suggests an error for either
Madley, north of Tamworth, or Tanworth in Warwickshire.

490 Smyth, Charles. The Art of Preaching. London: S.P.C.K.,
1940 (pp. 107, 114-117, 145-146, 167, 224).

Treats Taylor's use of exemplum and his advice on
preaching to his clergy in Ireland.

491 Stapelton, Laurence. The Elected Circle.
Princeton: Princeton Univ. Press, 1973 (passim).

Taylor is used as a contrast for a study of Donne's
sermons; Hazlitt's preference is for Taylor; DeQuincey's
comments are cited; and T. S. Eliot's interest in Taylor
on the subject of cadence is noted.

492 Stedmond, J. M. "English Prose of the Seventeenth
Century." Dalhousie Review, 30 (1950): 269-278.

General essay linking Milton's Areopagitica, Browne's
Hydriotaphia, and LP as typical of the poetic prose works
of the seventeenth century.

493 "V." [Untitled article]. Gentleman's Magazine,
61 (1791): 720.

Explains how the Archbishop of Canterbury came to hold
the advowson of Uppingham so that he could appoint
Taylor.

494 Warburton, William. Letters, ed. Richard Hurd.
New York: E. Sargeant, 1809 (pp. 92-95). [Letter L].

States that Taylor is oratorical as opposed to being a
discourser like Barrow and says his predeliction is
for Taylor.

495 Webb, Clement. "Blake and Jeremy Taylor." TLS,
April 11, 1929, p. 296.

Notes a similarity between "Auguries of Innocence" and
DD.

496 White, Helen C. English Devotional Literature.
Madison, Wisc.: Univ. of Wisconsin Press, 1930 (passim).

This excellent and wide-ranging study praises Taylor for
his style especially and his ability to direct attention
to material details as symbols of general truth and to
use all examples available to him--pagan as well as
Christian; also notes his insistence on the use of
reason and his attempt at the humanist work of bringing
order and moderation out of chaos and excess.

497 Williams, William P. "The Childrens Threes." AN&Q,
(1971): 83-84.

Notes the use of this phrase in John Cleveland's "A
Dialogue between two Zealots" and the use of the phrase
"jus trium liberorum" in LP and suggests a common
source for both of them.

498 Williams, William Proctor. "A Critical Old
Spelling Edition of Jeremy Taylor's Liberty of
Prophesying." DA, 29 (1969): 279-280. [Kansas
State U.].

S.E.

499 Williams, William P. "Eight Unpublished Letters by
Jeremy Taylor." Anglican Theological Review, 58 (1976):
179-193.

An old spelling edition, with notes, of these eight
letters from the Restoration, most to Archbishop
Bramhall.

500 Williams, William P. "Jeremy Taylor's Other Style."
Kansas Quarterly, 7 (1975): 91-96.

Points out that Taylor also possessed and used
effectively a forceful middle style and that he should
not be remembered only for his ornate style and purple
patches.

501 Willmott, Robert E. A. "S. T. Coleridge at Trinity."
Conversations at Trinity. London, 1836 (pp. 20-27).

Taylor is the Spenser of prose.

502 Wilson, F. P. Seventeenth-Century Prose.
Berkeley: Univ. of California Press, 1960 (pp. 5, 97,
102-103, 107-108).

Repeats the usual about Taylor's lack of great mental
powers and his ornate style's fall into disfavor after
the Restoration.

503 Woodall, Guy R. "James Russell Lowell's Works of
Jeremy Taylor, D. D." Costerus, 3 (1972): 221-236.

Notes Taylor's interest to Lowell through a study
of Lowell's copy of Heber's edition (No. 178).

Index of Authors

72

Index of Works

Date